AFTER GOD'S OWN HEART

Juliet Thomas

Pilot Books
Bromley

AFTER GOD'S OWN HEART
by Juliet Thomas

Published by
The Pilot Company
13 Warner Road
Bromley
Kent BR1 3RR
England

Cover design by Graham Turner

ISBN 1 85859 004 3

Printed by Cox and Wyman
Reading Berkshire

Acknowledgments
I am grateful to Nancy Morris for the wonderful job
she did in editing my papers

Chapter 1 of this book comprises the substance of
an address given by Juliet Thomas at the
Asian Conference for Evangelical Women which
was held in Singapore in 1989

Copies available in India from
O.M. Books
PO Box 2014
Secunderbad A P
India 500 003

CONTENTS

Chapter

A word about the author   8

Introduction   9

1   Liberated to serve   11

2   God's order for women   27

3   Ministries of some notable women   39

4   Prayer - the breath of Christian life   47

5   My personal experience   55

6   Women's role in evangelism   67

7   A call to action   83

A WORD ABOUT THE AUTHOR

Juliet Thomas is the Founder and Director of Arpana Ministries, a national prayer network in India. Arpana Ministries is a member of Operation Mobilisation. Juliet is part of the OM India Leadership Team and is much in demand as an international conference speaker.

She is a member of the Executive Committee of the Lausanne Convention and Chairperson of its Intercessory Group. She is also Vice Chairman of World Vision India. Married to Edison, a scientist, she has two grown-up children and is resident in Bangalore, India.

AFTER GOD'S OWN HEART

I first met Juliet Thomas in Manila in The Philippines at the Lausanne Congress in 1989. She was Chairperson of the plenary sessions for one day. I have a distinct memory of her leading us in prayer in a way that brought us all into deep "agreement" in that public prayer. I did not forget her.

Later, when Lausanne was looking for a Chairperson for its Intercession Working Group, in my role as International Director, I proposed her for the task and the Committee agreed and elected her. It is in that relationship that I have come to know and value Juliet.

She is her own person. Her ability to be like that comes from the freedom she has found in serving Jesus Christ. This comes out in her book *After God's Own Heart*. She tells it as it happened in her very candid autobiographical parts. There is no pretence. There is no overstatement. It rings true.

She has three passions; the godly family, prayer and sharing the Good News of Christ with others. I think they are in that order for her. In all of them she wants her sisters to play their God-given role to the full. She is pained when for any reason these areas of her interest are deprived of anything that women can bring to them.

So you will find the book a fascinating mixture of intriguing story, gripping imagery, personal philosophy and pointed exhortation. it will challenge you. You will have to think again about some things you thought were settled. You may not agree with all that she says, but you will read views that are lived and not only spoken.

As a man from the West, I deeply respect the pioneering she has done as a women from the great Sub-Continent that I never cease to admire.

I commend Juliet and her book to readers all over the world.

Tom Houston
Minister at Large of
The Lausanne Committee
for World Evangelisation.
August 17, 1994

Chapter one

Liberated to serve

Have you ever watched with wonder and awe, the breathtaking beauty of the breaking of a new day? The hatching of a chicken as it bursts forth from the egg that had held and nourished it till then? The birth of a baby, tiny and helpless and yet perfected in the very image of her creator God? I believe women are standing on the threshold of something that's wonderful - an awakening.

Something of this same awe grips my soul as I see women awaken as though from a long sleep to the uniqueness of our privileges and incredible potential that our loving God has called us to develop and use for His glory. We have been for too long bound by our own inhibitions, cultures and prejudices that have crippled us and hindered us from functioning in any capacity at all!

But now, the butterfly struggles out of her cocoon - painfully and slowly to come forth with the beauty and radiance that she has been created for! Woman, created in the image of God, redeemed by the precious blood of Christ, is joint-heir to the grace of life, co-inheritor of all the riches of the Kingdom of God. Would we ask for anything less? Would we attempt anything smaller for the glory of God? Would we not rather desire to stretch forth our wings and with courage and faith, rise up to all that God's Spirit entrusts us to do for the sake of the extension of His Kingdom!

May we with one heart and with one voice pray to our Lord God that He would indeed meet with us, that He would touch and transform each one of us, into vessels unto honour, meet for the Master's use. May our hearts therefore be open to hear Him speak afresh to us, so that we may be cleansed from anything that is impure. May our minds grasp yet again the magnitude of our calling not only to grow to fullness of the stature of Jesus Christ but to have His Word so burn within us that it becomes a compulsion for us to share Christ wherever we are and in whatever we do.

Woman:
In the plan and purpose of God

Woman was created by God as sharer in the same human nature as man. Both men and women were intended to show forth the image of God.

> "So God created man in His own image, in the image of God He created him; male and female He created them. God blessed them and said to them, 'Be fruitful and increase in number; fill the earth and subdue it. Rule over the fish of the sea and the birds of the air and over every living creature that moves on the gound.'" *Gen 1:27-28*

"Created in His image" which means that both male and female reflect the image and glory of God. We see humanity (male and female), in relation to God (they are in His image) and to nature (they are to fill the earth and subdue it). The stewardship of creation is given to both of them.

> "Then the Lord God said, 'It is not good for the man to be alone. I will make a helper suitable for him.'"
>
> *(Gen2:18)*

When God says "not good", He does not mean that He made a mistake or forgot something. The 'helper' for man is not someone whose place could conceivably have been filled by the animals or something else. Woman is made because she is needed. She complements man. She is neither extraneous or a luxury, not a nuisance or a hindrance, but a necessity for the welfare of man. Man is not made self-sufficient; he needs the woman's partnership for the fulfilment of God's purposes for him.

Thus woman enters the world designated by God as 'EZER KENEGDO' - helper fit for him. In the Old Testament, several times the word 'EZER' refers to God as the only effectual helper. So it can be safely said that it does not imply inferiority. More importantly the helper of man is 'KENEGDO', that is, 'corresponding to' or 'like him'. She corresponds to him in that she, like him, is made in the image of God.

Commenting on the special creation of Eve, Matthew Henry writes that she was 'not made out of his (Adam's) head to top him, or out of his feet to be trampled upon by him, but out of his side to be equal with him, under his arm to be protected, and near his heart to be loved'.

This primeval equality was, however, distorted by the fall. Part of God's judgement was His word to the woman;

> "Your desire will be for your husband, and he will
> rule over you" *(Gen 3:16)*.

Thus the dominance of man over woman, however first arrived at, is stated here, to be one of the effects of sin. That Jesus overcame sin is a promise that the effects of such sin will be eliminated through the grace-filled efforts of human beings. Christ's transforming power has been at work through the ages.

Thus, when one responds fully to divine grace there is a wonderful assurance of sins forgiven; the heart is clean, the soul is free. Faith no longer staggers at the promises of God.

Bernard of Clairvaux, correctly called Mary Magdalene 'the apostle to the apostles'. She witnessed the life and death of Jesus, His burial and resurrection. She was sent to the disciples to proclaim the Easter 'KERYGMA'. So we as women today may rediscover the important function and role which we have in the Christian faith and community.

> "But you" (this includes us women too!) "will be
> my witnesses in Jerusalem, and all Judea and
> Samaria and to the ends of the earth" *Acts 1:8*.

It is like tossing a pebble into the lake, isn't it? We throw ourselves into being God's witnesses where we are, and the waves we make reach far. The woman begins with her family and others close to her.

Catherine Booth, mother of the famous Booth family of the Salvation Army, was once heard to pray, 'O God I will not stand before Thee without my family', and God saved the whole Booth family and gave them a marvellous ministry.

"Believe on the Lord Jesus and you will be saved - you and your household" *Acts 16:31*.

My study of the scriptures, and the lessons drawn from church growth in places like Korea and China, impress upon me that the Lord's pattern for biblical evangelism primarily is the Christian home. The home can only become God's means of reaching others if it is Christ-honouring, and obedient in practical living to the teaching of the scriptures. These homes become centres of discipling and outreach. The Lord works powerfully through them to bring His healing to a hurting world.

Woman:
Her problems and prejudices in our culture

Dr. John Stott, in his analysis 'Women, Men and God' writes:

> "There is no doubt that in many cultures women have habitually been despised and demeaned by men. They have often been treated as mere playthings and sex objects, as unpaid cooks, housekeepers and child-minders, and as brainless simpletons incapable of engaging in rational discussion. Their gifts have been unappreciated, their personality smothered, their freedom curtailed, and their service in some areas exploited, in others refused." *Issues Facing Christians Today*

In her book *Feminist Theology as a Critical Theology of Liberation*, Elizabeth Schussler Florenza writes:

> "Women are not allowed to be independent and free human persons. They are not supposed to ex-

press their own opinion, but to be silent and voice only that of the fathers, husbands, bosses or sons.

"Someone has graphically described the plight of women in our society thus:

Woman

   Bent over by the weight of the world
family. . . society. . . church
   never allowed to stand straight.
Bent over by loads of bricks
   of stone. . . of water. . . of baskets of wares.
Bending over the fireplace
   the washing stone. . . the ironing board. . .
   the grinding stone.
Bent over by racism
   caste. . . religion. . . and class.
Bent over by unjust structures
   social. . . political. . . economic. . . cultural
never allowed to stand straight.
Woman bent over under the fury of
   a husband's rage. . . a capitalist's greed. . .
   a landlord's lust. . .
a cruel world's dictate.
Woman is
   not meant to. . . not supposed to. . .
   not allowed to stand straight.
Woman broken inside
Spiritually abused and diseased
derided, bullied, beaten - even burnt to death!
depressed, miserable, thinking nothing of herself,
believing that her destiny is her bent-over state."

In Christ

When we focus our attention on Christ however, we are reminded that the gospels present Christ as appreciating the distinct capabilities of women. Early in His ministry Jesus opened the doors to intimate affinity with Himself, gender constituted no barrier to this intimacy. Women thus became active workers for His Kingdom, and His valued disciples.

> "For whoever does the will of my Father in heaven is my brother and sister and mother."
>
> *(Matt 12:50, Mark 3:35, Luke 8:21)*

People think that we can put our identity in circumstances or functions. But these circumstances and functions can change and then we are thrown off balance, confused. We must place our identity in that which will not change - even Jesus Christ. Thus establishing our identity in Christ no matter what our feelings or inadequacies may be, no matter what circumstances we may be called to face, no matter what voices are raised against us, through it all we stand secure in Him, free, liberated to let God work His gracious purposes in and through us. Our 'little' place in God's hands, becomes much!

No power on earth can deter the mighty advance of the gospel when the Holy Spirit is permitted to equip and empower His people, both men and women, for evangelism.

> "The Lord announced the word; and great was the company of those who proclaimed it:"
>
> *(Psalm 68:11)*

In the Church

In the 19th century the church pioneered the education of women. They were trained as doctors and nurses to treat other women. Though the church pioneered these reforms in society, she has never fully opened her own doors to women. Cultural attitudes rather than biblical attitudes towards women have dominated the church, in Asia.

> "I would have given the church my head, my heart, my hand. She would not have them. She did not know what to do with them. She told me to go back and crochet in my mother's drawing room; or marry and look well at the head of my husband's table. 'You may go to Sunday school if you like it', she said. But she gave me no training or education for it."

This woman went on to organise health and sanitation for the British Army and the adjacent local villages in India, and her knowledge of the country was such that several Viceroys even went to her for briefing before taking up their duties. She planned the development of district nursing in the whole district of Lancashire and the first training school for nurses in Britain. Her name was Florence Nightingale. "And it's doubtful whether even today her church would know what to do with her God-given gifts! And she was not alone in her frustration," says Valerie Griffiths, "for in the mid-19th century, thousands of middle-class women did nothing."

The Asian church needs to recover her heritage. The women in Asia, in spite of our cultural inhibitions and natural timidity, need to be enabled to function fully and effectively within the body of Christ. In most of our churches latent talent and godly ability are dormant. Without encouragement and direction, teaching and training, even the most gifted will achieve little.

'It is profoundly disturbing to face the possibility that over a long period of time the church may have been denying to women the place assigned to them by God. But there is no growth without pain and struggle and in this area as in others, the church must come to maturity.'

It is true, "The church is God's agent in the earth - the medium through which He expresses Himself to the world". Could we then seriously ask ourselves whether the reason God has not been able to fully express Himself to the world; the reason the church is not marching forward in Christ's mission in the world, is because she is not a fully functioning church? She is handicapped and crippled, particularly because the tremendous potential and possibilities of women have not been developed.

Woman: Her potential and possibilities

What is a woman worth? According to the materialist - not much! According to the Indian value system, a woman is a liability - not an asset at all!

She esteems her worth

The Bible says a woman's value is far above precious jewels. On the authority of God's Word we can therefore confidently affirm that a woman is priceless.

I once heard an interesting story of how God created woman. A Sunday school teacher told her class of little girls about the creation of Adam and Eve. Afterwards, she asked the class to write the story on a piece of paper. One little girl wrote, "God created Adam out of the dust of the earth. . ." Then she paused for she had forgotten what happened next. Not to be outdone, she continued, "God then looked at Adam and said, 'Surely I can do better than that'. . . and so He created Eve"!

Women generally do not share the self-confidence of this little girl! For low self-image rates as the number one cause of depression in women according to findings of a famous psychologist. Listen to what we often hear from women: 'Isn't that just like me to do such a stupid thing!' 'Oh no, I can't do this.' 'If only I can be as calm and capable as she is.' But when we women begin to have the divine perspective about ourselves and others, then we can productively minister in Christ's Name.

The woman who responds to God's love with all her heart and soul and mind will walk tall and straight as a daughter of the King. She will be released from the torment of low self-image and the fears that cripple her from sharing the Good News. Instead she will reach out in love to her neighbours - as a healing agent where people are hurting, as a catalyst for change where wrongs need to be righted, and a prophetic voice where God's word for the hour needs to be heard.

She exercises her gifts

God's plan for the world involves having people utilise

the talents He has given them. "Unused gifts waste the grace of God and choke spiritual life, both personally and corporately", says Pamela Heim. How true that "learning your gifts will take time. Using your gift will take the rest of your life."

In *The Truth About You* we read:

> "Can you begin to imagine how the world would benefit if people were educated and employed on the basis that each person is gifted? Regardless of how old or young you are - how low on the totem pole you see yourself - how impoverished your education or upbringing - you have been given good gifts. You have been designed and have a role to play that will fulfil you and please others. Discover your design!"

Dr John Stott affirms:

> "There is a general presumption in favour of women in ministry (including leadership and teaching). It is that on the Day of Pentecost, in fulfilment of prophecy, God poured out His Spirit on 'all flesh', including 'sons and daughters' and His servants, both men and women. If the gift of the Spirit was bestowed on all believers of both sexes, so were His gifts. There is no evidence, or even hint, that the charismata were restricted to men. On the contrary, the Spirit's gifts were distributed to all for the common good, making possible what is often called 'every member ministry of the Body of Christ'.

> "We must conclude therefore, not only that Christ

gives charismata (including the teaching gifts) to women, but that alongside His gifts He issues His call to develop and exercise them in His service and in the service of others, for the building up of His Body." *(Issues Facing Christians Today)*

The Lord is building His church. But how can He build, how can the church rise while the gifts of three-quarters of her membership are sepulchred in her midst?

> *Daughters of Zion, from the dust*
> *Exalt thy fallen head;*
> *Again in thy Redeemer trust*
> *He calls thee from the dead.*

She fulfils her mission

Susan T Foh, in her book *Women and the Word of God*, concludes as follows:

"Today, there is forbidden fruit just as there was in the Garden. That fruit is role-interchangeability in marriage, church and society. Christian women, like Eve, are being tempted with half truths (such as subordination implies inferiority) and are being told that God (or the Bible or the church) is depriving them of something quite arbitrarily. (We forget that God's commandments are for our own good.) In some instances Christian women are deceived into thinking that God's Word forbids more than it does; they think they must not even touch the tree with the forbidden fruit. And like Eve, Christian women are guilty of sinning against their Creator by discussing with other creatures whether or not God's law is fair."

Men and women are told:

> "The world over, people today are hungry for more than bread. They are hungry for the Bread of Life which comes from a right relationship with the living God."

In this 'me' generation, too many women are pre-occupied by their own needs. It is important that we reassess our own priorities and rededicate ourselves to the task. Michael Green describes women who 'gossiped Christianity at the laundry' and he suggests that these women were among the most successful evangelists.

Who can name the vast number of women listed in God's Honour Roll and the glories of many more who are unnamed and unsung? Who can evaluate their precious contribution of life and labour, faith and service, often through severe pain and struggle that people may be blessed and the Lord's Name be glorified? Is there any telling what God can do with one woman who is totally dedicated and surrendered to Him? 'A holy woman is an awesome weapon in the hand of God'.

Women in the ranks of the Quakers, others like Susanna Wesley, Madam Guyon, Mary Slessor, Catherine Booth, Pandita Ramabai, Amy Carmichael and many more have blazed the trail before us. And yet. . . and yet we are slow to follow in their footsteps! Why? I believe there are two major reasons.

First, it is the self-oppression of women themselves who do not seriously believe God is willing to penetrate the inner springs of human character and begin a solitary revolution there - that God can and needs to work through the likes of us.

Second, it is suppression from without, due to the attitudes of our culture, society and surprisingly, in many places, the church. In *Women and Quakerism* by Hope Elizabeth Luder, George Fox is quoted as trying to explain men's reactions to women in ministry by saying that perhaps they felt threatened. But men 'need not fear anyone is getting over them, for the power and Spirit of God gives liberty to all', said Fox. Women need to be careful as an attitude of arrogance or resentment may well provoke the resistance and wrath of men.

It is my earnest prayer and plea that in this age as women seek recognition and visibility that in so doing we may be clothed in humility, modesty, and womanly dignity. Let us beware we do not lose our unique graces of femininity God has specially created us with. How wonderful when brothers and sisters together in the family of God work for the upbuilding of one another - not competing but complementing! The gifts and potential of each are released thus fulfilling Christ's mission through the church and the world today!

You too may 'have come into the kingdom for a time such as this'. God has put you where you are to be salt, to be a witness. Prepare yourself with prayer and fasting, and like Esther who, with undaunted courage, spurred by her immense confidence in her God and intense love of her people, went forth to meet the King with the words 'And if I perish, I perish'! Where are God's Esthers today?

Woman: Her passion and compassion

This is a time of unparalleled harvest for the kingdom of

God. We are living in the computer age and in an instant society. Today our environment is shouting a message to us. Can we hear the message? Can we see the symptoms? Our society in many ways is coming apart at the seams. There is no more time to be passive and indifferent. We need to move. But we cannot allow the excitement of the harvest and the wonder of the modern age to cloud our senses and move us too quickly until we have waited upon God for wisdom and direction. Pray that the Lord of the harvest will thrust forth more and more women labourers into His vineyard.

Lift up your eyes and see! Do you see the crying needs of women all around us? Do you feel their pain and pressure in your very soul? Have you and I any understanding of the agony of women abused, exploited and oppressed? Or have we become accustomed to these common sights and scenes? God forbid!

We are fully aware of the rising staggering statistics of rape, prostitution, dowry deaths, drug addictions, idolatries and immoralities, illiteracy, poverty, battered wives, divorce, female foeticide, child abuse, bonded labour, plight of women prisoners, pornography, etc. To our shame, too often these find more response and compassion from non-Christians than from us Christian women! And yet should it not be we who have been touched and transformed by the love of Christ, who can bring effective healing to these multitudes that are hurting all around us? Let us not be diverted or deterred or entangled in controversies and squabbles over the thorny issues of status and role of women! Let us with a sense of urgency get on with our unfinished task!

Jabez called on the God of Israel saying,

> "Oh that you would. . . enlarge my territory. Let your hand be with me and keep me from harm so that I will be free from pain." *(1 Chron 4:10)*

And God granted him that which he requested.

If the Lord is in it, there will be painful but exciting growth and He will stretch us as He enlarges our 'territory'. He will also do the extraordinary as we allow Him to lead us one step at a time. . . knowing that He goes before.

May our heart-cry these days be 'Lord stir the flames of revival - and begin in me'! May this Conference be used of God as a springboard to propel us forth in ever widening circles to reach Asia for Christ. May the Spirit of God equip and empower you and me to be 'God's women in Asia' - the women with 'the bent knees, and wet eyes and broken hearts'. Amen.

Chapter two

God's order for women

In Creation

In today's world women are taking an increasingly active and dominant role in society. For the past few years many women in the church have become restless? "Why doesn't the church extend equal rights to women as to men?" they demand. Francis A Schaeffer in his book *True Spirituality* says, "When one hears the cry 'I am not equal to others', in reality the cry means, 'I want to be better than others and am not'." He adds that for the Christian, status and validity do not rest upon relative relationships to other people. As a Christian, my validity and status are found in my being before God.

It is important for us to look closely at this role-relationship. What does the Bible and the church teach? How should we elect officers of the church, and conduct public worship? What is the biblical teaching on marriage and family relationships? We need to discern what is our cultural inheritance, and what is biblical teaching. Sometimes they are the same, often not. Can we accept the Bible if it seems to go against our cultural norms?

The crucial question is therefore: "What is the status and role of a woman as given to her by God as taught in the scriptures?" It is so easy to be tempted to take a view that enjoys greater popularity and which may be more in keeping with our cultural norms. But we need to know and obey what God is speaking to us through His Word. So, with an open mind and prayerful heart I have grappled with this question. I have read as widely as I can and have prayerfully studied the scriptures.

At the risk of repeating myself I want to look again at the book of Genesis.

The earliest reference we have is in the first chapter of the first book of the Bible. In Genesis 1:27 we read "So God created man in His own image, in the image of God He created him, male and female He created them." Then a little further on in Genesis 5:1-2 "When God created man, He made him in the likeness of God. Male and female He created them and He blessed them and named them 'man'".

Note the phrase "created in His own image" which means that male and female alike reflect or bear the image and glory of God. Together, they share in the divine blessings. Now when we look at the revealed facts concerning God, we see that He is the Triune God (see John 1:1 and 2 Corinthians 13:14). Our God is Father, Son and Holy Spirit. Each person of the Trinity has the same substance and essence of being God. (Philippians 2:6 and John 14:9-11.) Yet in the Godhead we see a clear order and relationship within this Trinity. Each person of the Trinity plays a different role. The Father sends the Son (John 3:17). The Son, in perfect obedience to His Father, goes to His death on the cross (Philippians 2:6-8). When the Son rose from the dead, He ascended to the Father and sent the Holy Spirit into our world (John 16:7). The work of God the

Holy Spirit is to glorify God the Son (John 16:12-15).

Here we see a perfect picture of equality and unity but also of obedience and submission. There is a clear relationship and order between the three Persons of the Triune God. In the same way we find that in human beings created in His image there is meant to be an order and relationship.

If we can look back at Genesis 5:2 for a minute, we note that it says "He blessed *them* and called them man". God called them – that is both of them – "man". It was man who said "She shall be called 'woman' for she was taken out of man" (Genesis 2:23). In God's sight, when God created man and woman, they were absolutely equal.

As we will see, God created them equal but with different roles. Just as it is with His own nature. The Father, Son and Holy Spirit are all equal but with different roles to play.

In the home

In Genesis 2:18 we read "It is not good for the man to be alone. I will make a helper *suitable for him*". In Genesis 2:22, "Then the Lord God made a woman from the rib he had taken out of the man, and he brought her to the man". In Genesis 3:16, ". . . your desire will be for your husband and he will rule over you".

I often used to wonder at the purpose God had in creating woman out of man. After all, He created everything else out of nothing, and created man himself out of the dust of the ground. But He created woman out of man. This speaks to me of the intimate, unique *interdepen-*

dence and order in the relationship of one with the other! They are truly a complement of each other, the one perfecting and completing the other in love and harmony but never in rivalry and competition. This was and is God's purpose. Man to be the natural leader and woman to be his natural helpmate. Co-equal in the sight of God, but with clearly defined and differing roles to play.

Let us look for a moment at two rather difficult scriptures, two verses that do not fit very easily with our modern Western culture, and that even in the East are being found increasingly difficult:

1 Corinthians 11:3, "Now I want you to realise that the head of every man is Christ, and the head of the woman is man and the head of Christ is God".

1 Corinthians 11:8, "For man did not come from woman but woman from man, neither was man created for woman, but woman for man".

If what these verses say is true, and we certainly believe it is, then there is a clear division or biblical order for the family. This order is that the man is the head and the woman his submissive partner. Every human being is of equal worth, whether a man or a woman, yet with different roles to fulfil. Unfortunately, many people think, and even teach, that submissiveness shows inferiority. It is not so, but in many cultures, especially in my Eastern culture, we have been taught that a woman is inferior to a man. This is not what the Bible teaches. For we see in the Trinity not only perfect equality and unity but also perfect obedience and submissiveness. The Son submitted to the Father but was in no way inferior. Likewise a woman submitting to a man does not make her inferior.

To counterbalance the wrong cultural teaching that is so often given in our society that submission means inferiority, some modern writers focus on the necessity for equality in the male/female relationship and presume that this rules out all differences of function in the role relationship. They like to point out Galatians 3:28 "There is neither Jew nor Greek, slave nor free, male nor female, for you are all one in Christ Jesus" and argue that this means that there is to be no submission of women to men either in the marriage relationship or in the ruling or teaching functions in the church.

I disagree. I believe that equality and difference of role are not mutually exclusive but are indeed like two sides of a coin, the two sides to the teaching of the Word of God on the subject. It is significant that the apostle Peter appeals to the husband to honour his wife as a "fellow-heir" (1 Peter 3:7) - that is, as his equal. He also urges the husband to recognise his wife's femininity (as the weaker vessel) and the wife to submit to her husband. Likewise, the apostle Paul writes of man and woman as one in Christ (Galatians 3:28) and also writes of the wife's submission to the headship of her husband (Ephesians 5:22; Colossians 3:18-19). Equality and role difference are compatible.

Let me illustrate it this way. Can you imagine an office unit functioning with two heads? There will be utter chaos as each will try to run it her own way and impose her own will. Therefore, for the office to function effectively, though the two may be of equal rank, one must assume leadership and the other will need to submit to her authority. Likewise in the family unit, though husband and wife have equal status before God, for the proper functioning of the family in God's plan and order, the husband assumes *headship not lordship* and the wife submits to his authority in the Lord.

Ephesians 5:22, "Wives submit to your husbands as to the Lord. For the husband is the head of the wife, as Christ is the head of the church".

Colossians 3:18, "Wives submit to your husbands as is fitting in the Lord".

1 Peter 3:1, "Wives, in the same way be submissive to your husbands".

I can confirm this from my own experience. Being of a proud and independent nature, the fallen nature within me rebelled at this idea of submission. But praise God that redeemed in Christ, by His grace I learned submission to my husband. I can attest now that there can be no more beautiful, richer, deeper relationship than the marriage relationship where this order of God is followed. I have not become my husband's slave. I have a clearly defined role of my own before God.

We need to note that when a doctrine or principle written in the Old Testament, as this one is, is confirmed by the Lord (in Mark 10:6-8) and apostles in the New Testament (as stated above) then this is binding for all time and is not meant to be interpreted differently for different ages, cultures and situations.

In the Church

Elizabeth Elliot points out, "The church must choose between ordination and subordination of women - if subordination is the command of God, ordination is excluded and this exclusion of women from ordination is based on the order established in creation".

With this in mind, let us look at a couple of the most disputed passages in scripture to find out the God-appointed role and ministry of women in the church.

1 Corinthians 14:34-35, "As in all the churches of the saints, the woman should keep silence in churches. For they are not permitted to speak, but should be subordinate as even the law says. If there is anything they desire to know let them ask their husbands at home. It is sinful for a woman to speak in the church".

1 Timothy 2:11-12, "Let a woman learn in silence. I permit no woman to teach or to have authority over men . . . for Adam was first formed then Eve. . ."

This injunction is given in the context of Paul's remarks about holding an office in the church, i.e. Bishops, Elders, Pastors, etc. Paul explains in 1 Timothy 5:17 that the role of the Bishop/Elder is to have authority and to teach. This is the authority of person and office. Women are reminded that in recognising God's order in the church, the pastorate is not to be their role. Nowhere in the New Testament is there any record of women in such an office and this, as we shall see later, is definitely not because of lack of notable, gifted and godly women in the church.

It is true that we must not confuse what is local and temporary with what is universal and permanent. But embedded in what is said are principles which we are to apply to situations everywhere. In the above mentioned verses, 1 Timothy 2:11-12, Paul does not merely use cultural arguments but goes back to grasp the principle of

33

God's order in creation. "A woman should learn in quietness and full submission."

So we see that women are told to learn in quietness. In 'quietness' suggests a spirit of meekness rather than aggressiveness, and does not mean that she should never open her mouth in church. Rev. Ian Kemp points out that this same expression is used in 2 Thessalonians 3:12 (AV) of men who are to work and eat their own bread 'in quietness'. It does not suggest that they should never speak while working, but rather diligently and without disturbance to others, they should apply themselves to the task. However, 'learning in silence' does not exclude women from praying and prophesying in the church (1 Corinthians 11:5). We conclude therefore that as in the home so in the church, the official leadership is not to be hers. This subordination mentioned does not exclude the absolute equality before God of both woman and man.

Galatians 3:28, "There is neither Jew nor Greek, slave nor free, male nor female; for you are all one in Christ Jesus". This text, taken in the light of its context, is used to claim equality of the sexes with regard to their roles. It addresses the question 'who may become a son of God and on what basis'. It answers that any person, regardless of race, sex or civil status, may do so by faith in Christ. The gospel is for everyone.

Paul is therefore not reflecting upon relationships within the body of Christ. He was thinking about the basis of membership in the body. This means that it is an error to say that 'all one' in Christ means that there are no distinctions within the body. When we speak of allowing all men to join the army, we do not mean that there will be no distinction between the tank corps and the infantry team. It does not mean that all will be goalies or full-backs on a football team. A military or sporting analogy has certain drawbacks when applied to the body of Christ. Yet it is inescapable that Paul himself did not seem to feel any tension between his proclamation that all are one in Christ, and his teaching that the one body of Christ has many different members. He also taught that his own authority was distinctive and all who would not acknowledge it should not be acknowledged (Galatians 3:28; 1 Corinthians 12:12 and 14:37-38).

It is worthwhile noticing that the apostle Peter seems to have shared Paul's view with respect to the sexes. In 1 Peter 3:1-7, he speaks of the unity of the male and female marriage partners as 'heirs together of the gracious gift of life'. (AV) In precisely this context he calls for a role differentiation between the spouses. It would thus appear that Paul's willingness to see that unity in Christ is not undercut by distinctions between believers is not unique to him, but more widely shared in the early Christian community.

A note in Paul's defence. . . There are some who argue that Paul was an "anti-feminist, the arch-tyrant of sex discrimination, the preacher of female inferiority". They say that it is *he* who binds women in the scriptures. In the context of the same verses mentioned above (1 Corinthians 14:34-35), Paul writes in 1 Corinthians 14:37, "If anybody thinks he is a prophet or spiritually gifted, let him acknowledge that what I am writing to you is the Lord's command." And if it is the command of the Lord, we should obey it.

Secondly, a reasonable study of scripture shows that Paul was far from anti-feminist. He had the greatest regard and respect for women, and gave them great dignity unheard of elsewhere at that time. Let us not forget that this same Paul writes in 1 Corinthians 11:12, "In the Lord however, woman is not independent of man, nor is man independent of woman. For as woman came from man; so also man is born of woman. But everything comes from God".

Thirdly, Paul was a realist and a fervent evangelist. In his words he had become all things to all men that by all means he might win some. If out-moded customs or crippling tradition hindered the advancement of the gospel, would he not be the first to discard them?

Jesus' attitude to women

Someone has well said that each individual gospel records the powerful impression produced upon women by the personality and teaching of Jesus. This impression could only have been made by one who had a sincere belief in the intellectual and spiritual possibilities of women. Jesus showed appreciation of women's spiritual capability and her ability to serve. There can be no doubt that as regards spiritual privilege, Jesus considered the two sexes equal. However, as regard spiritual activity, there was a difference between that of man and woman. What is not said about women is as important as what is said.

Jesus Christ opened the privilege of religious faith equally to men and women. He gave His message publicly and privately to women as well as to men. It is, however, significant that Jesus chose and sent out 70 men. It is significant that there was no woman chosen among the 12 disciples. It is significant that the Lord's Supper was instituted in the presence of men only. (It is to be remembered that the occasion was also the celebration of the Passover.) It is significant that the apostolic commission John 20:19-23 and Matthew 28:16-20 was given to men only.

It is argued, however, that Christ did not choose women because of the cultural climate, social mentality and prevailing customs of His time. But did Christ really conform to cultural and social problems? No, because His attitude towards women was quite different from that commonly held and He deliberately and courageously broke from it. Among Persians, Greeks and Jews alike, a man used to give thanks that he was not an unbeliever or uncivilised, that he was not a woman and not a slave.

But Jesus did not conform to culture as we see in John 4:27, where He dared to speak publicly to a Samaritan woman so that even the apostles were amazed at Him.

In Matthew 9:20-22 we find a woman who is bleeding. Jesus takes no notice of her state of legal impurity but allows her to touch His garment and, instead of rebuking her, He commends her faith.

In Luke 7:37 He allows a 'sinful' woman to approach Him in the house of Simon the Pharisee.

In John 8:11, when the men were ready to stone an adulterous woman, Jesus points out that they should not be more severe towards the faults of women than that of men.

In Matthew 19:3 and 9; Mark 10:2 and 11, Jesus does not hesitate to depart from the Mosaic law to affirm the equality of the rights and duties of men and women with regard to the marriage bond.

Moreover, in His itinerant ministry, Jesus was accompanied not only by His 12 apostles but also by a group of women (Luke 8:1-3). Yet Jesus chose only men. He obviously did this on purpose and thereby fixed a norm. This does not mean that women had no place in the ministry. Even in Jesus' time, they did. They often showed a devotion that surpassed men and Jesus had words of the highest praise for them.

Therefore, we must accept the fact that as men and women we are:

- equal in worth before God but different in roles
- equal in privileges in Christ but different in spiritual activities

Chapter three

Ministries of some notable women

Let me briefly sketch some ways leading women were used to God's glory in the Bible:

In the Old Testament

Deborah (Judges 4): She was the leader of her nation Israel. A woman who, although first among her people, did not 'boss' it over Barak – but placed herself next to Barak encouraging his faint heart and feeble hands to fulfil God's purposes for their nation. No thought of rivalry, position or competition was there in her mind. She claimed no honour for herself but through tactful spiritual leadership she made a strong leader of the man Barak. Where are the Deborahs in the body of Christ?

Huldah (2 Chronicles 34:22-28): A housewife. Her husband Shallum was in charge of King Josiah's wardrobe. She was a prophetess and it was to her that Hilkiah the High Priest, Shaphan the secretary, and other VIP's came to discover God's will concerning the Book of the Law which Hilkiah had found in the temple. Why was she consulted instead of the prophet Jeremiah? God needed a human being to speak His Word and He chose this woman who was available and in communion with Him.

God's tools often are the humble, weak, and frail things of this world – so that the glory will be His alone. Huldah did not exercise any authority by her person or office but she did demonstrate the authority of the Word of God. There is never any place for dominance in the church.

In the New Testament

Phoebe (Romans 16:1-2): She was entrusted by Paul to carry his letter to the Christians in Rome. Was she a deaconess who gave only unofficial service? We do not know. We do know, however, that she was a 'servant of the church' and that was all that mattered.

Priscilla (Acts 18:1-2, 18-19, 26 and 16:2): She formed a beautiful team relationship with her husband Aquila, the tent-maker. Paul, calling her Prisca in his letter to the Romans, shows that he held her with deep esteem and affection as 'a dear sister in the Lord'. As Eugene Price says, 'Priscilla was able to use the wonderful mind God had given her in total submission to the Lord God who held the central place in her creative and fruitful life'. Since men always held the place of honour in society in Priscilla's time, it is unique that in the Bible her name is usually mentioned before her husband's name.

Yet Priscilla was no domineering woman. She was without conceit or domination, indeed she possessed a rare ability to lead without offending or displaying herself. Look at the harmony that must have existed between Priscilla and her husband. She must have understood her quiet and reserved husband and it is a tribute to her ability in handling relationships that he could follow her leadership without feeling inferior. In Acts 18:26 this is also demonstrated in the case of Apollos, the gifted orator, whom she and Aquila straightened out on his doctrine without offending him.

I have deliberately picked out these women. They are often quoted to support the election of women to official leadership in the church. Yet God was able to use them to fulfil His plan and purpose for His people because of their spirit of meekness, gentleness and submissiveness.

How much more, if we had the time, could we say of the many women who have tirelessly and selflessly toiled for their Lord down through the ages!

The 'ordination' of women

I have taken part in various discussions and debates on women's ordination and it has troubled me a great deal to see the attitude in which women fight for their so called rights and the degrading manner in which some men try to put them down! We need so much to remind ourselves again that we need to 'have the mind of Christ' in us. We should not aim for position and power but be ready for service and sacrifice. We should not look for positions that are merely men appointed, but service that is Spirit directed and done whole-heartedly as unto the Lord.

It is also to be regretted that many of the arguments, discussions and articles on this issue are held and written without any attempt to understand the Will of God through the study of the Word of God. Rather, arguments are based on history, social culture and changing trends in society. Not that these should not be taken into consideration. Our authority and standard should be the Bible, allowing scripture to interpret scripture.

Furthermore, it is obvious that the demand for women to be ordained and made priests of God is due to the direct influence of secular culture. They point to this as a progressive step, as in society today women have effectively invaded every field of activity and service. They argue that in the religious sphere women should not be barred from ordination and official leadership. Does this mean that the church should follow the world? Is this in keeping with the teaching of the Word of God? Can the unchanging Word become the changeable Word that must square with a changing culture which now has become the norm for life?

Firstly, should it not be the other way around? Is not the Lord building His church in the world in order that society may be touched and transformed through her clear witness? Her call is to be the 'salt of the earth' and the 'light of the world'. The explicit command of God throughout the Old Testament and the New Testament to His people is to be holy. That is to be set apart for God, a 'peculiar people', a distinctive community of God's people. We need to be warned again *not to be conformed to this world* – or to allow the world to squeeze us into its mould – but to *be transformed* (Romans 12:2). In these days the church is in danger of being swept away by the world, its standards and values and, thereby losing her identity.

Secondly, how has this emancipation or liberation of women affected society? God has given me a special burden for families, for in the society of today we find the tragic break-up of many homes. To a great extent, social and economic pressures have played their destructive roles. But the root cause is, I believe, because *women have stepped out of the line and order God has given for them*.

Consider her attitudes to those entrusted to her in the home, her sense of priorities, her struggle to be equal in all respects and in every area to man who is her counterpart. She has, in the conflict, lost her identity, her dignity and her respect. This identity crisis is so prevalent in the West that it is becoming an accepted thing for two men to live together as a married couple! Should these abominations and disrupting influences find an echo in the church? God forbid! *If the family unit – the basic and most important unit of the church and society – is to be preserved, then women must find and fit into their rightful place in the home, in the church and in society.*

All around us today we keep hearing cries of liberation. One among those is 'women's liberation'. This they claim will solve the problem of exploitation and oppression of women, rape and dowry death, etc. But will it really? Exploitation and oppression of women are caused by the evil thoughts, greed and wickedness of man. That is why these atrocities against women still occur. In fact, they are worse in the West where women enjoy their rights and equality! These can only be stopped when men's hearts and minds are cleansed by the transforming power of the living Lord.

Women today, due to cultural inhibitions and natural timidity, have not been able to function fully and effectively within the body of Christ. Many of the gifts of the Holy Spirit are for all God's children, men and women. "To prepare God's people for works of service, so that the body of Christ may be built up" (Ephesians 4:12). But the gifts given to women have hardly been used. Women need to be encouraged to awaken to the fact that they do possess gifts which need to be developed within the body for the total and effective functioning of the church.

Acts 2:17-18, "In the last days, God says, I will pour out my Spirit on all people. Your sons and daughters will prophesy, your young men will see visions, your old men will dream dreams. Even on my servants, both men and women, I will pour out my Spirit in those days and they will prophesy".

The many ways in which women can minister must be envisaged and developed within the church. But the ministry of women cannot and should not be equated with the ordination of women.

My Bible dictionary states, "In the Christian understanding of ministry is the rendering of a lowly but loving service to God and man". Also, in the words of Hort, Christ lifted 'every grade and pattern of service into a higher sphere. . . administration thus became one of the primary aims of Christian actions and the generic term is applied to all forms of ministry within the church'.

Speaking from personal experience, in our church our pastors have been encouraged to develop the lay leadership as much as possible. Thus we find women involved in every area of service: leading Bible studies and prayer groups, visiting the sick, counselling, teaching Sunday School, helping the Youth Fellowship and the young professionals, distributing to the needy, keeping open homes, amongst several other things. We also have been encouraged to take an active part in our worship services even to the sharing of God's Word. Truly, we women have an effective supportive ministry in our church.

Thus, this is an appeal to pastors and Christian leaders. God has given women a tremendous capacity for love, understanding and work. There are a great number of gifted and godly women who can help pastors turn the tide of broken homes that is sweeping into our churches. They need to be awakened to their responsibilities and encouraged to develop and use their God-given gifts in the body. Many problems can be worked out as women learn from women to be better wives and better mothers and thus better members of their church and better citizens of their country.

May God enable each one of us to think with the mind of Christ, to love with the heart of Christ and to serve in the Spirit of Christ in unity and harmony for the upholding of His body the church and for the glory of His Name among other peoples.

Chapter four

Prayer - the breath of Christian life

I am involved in building a national network of praying women in India, and our aim is to penetrate our nation with prayer. Also to stand with others in prayer for the nation that God may bring people to Himself.

I want to share a little bit, not about what to pray for, or how to pray, but to share with you some of the lessons the Lord has been teaching me in this area.

Prayer is not an exercise, it is not a programme, it is not even a certain mechanical form of posture. Prayer, I have learned, is a way of life. Prayer is the very breath of our soul. If we talk of physical life as breathing as vital for the life processes of the body, so is prayer the vital core of, the very life of, our spirits. Prayer is like breathing: i.e. breathing in, breathing out.

Prayer is therefore a heart communion with God himself. In prayer, I learn to pulse rate with the very heartbeat of God. I learn to grieve over the things that grieve and break God's heart. Prayer is therefore a pre-occupation of the soul with God.

I want to look at a few verses from one of the passages in scripture through which God has constantly spoken. A passage with which I go to the Lord quite often, and that is found in Revelation 2:2-5.

"I know your deeds, your hard work and your perseverance. I know that you cannot tolerate wicked men, that you have tested those who claim to be apostles but are not, and have found them false. You have persevered and have endured hardships for my name, and have not grown weary. Yet I hold this against you: You have forsaken your first love. Remember the height from which you have fallen! Repent and do the things you did at first. If you do not repent, I will come to you and remove your lampstand from its place."

A familiar passage. This is the first message that the risen Lord Jesus Christ gives to John. The first of the seven messages to the churches. We find that when something is said once, it is important enough - when it is said twice it is more important, but here we find one verse in Revelation chapters 2- 3 repeated seven times. This is the verse that we see at the end of every message that Christ gives, 'He who has an ear, let him hear what the Spirit says to the churches'.

We find, therefore, that it is very important for us as a people of God to listen to what the Spirit is saying. God is continually speaking to us, in many and varied ways. But the question I want to ask myself and I ask you is - are we listening? Yes, are we listening? "He who has an ear, let him hear what the Spirit says". It is so easy for us, is it not, to tune out what God is saying. We are good at talking - and often our prayer time is only talking to God. In fact, we often seem to be saying - 'listen Lord, for your servant speaks'!

The church in Ephesus is commended for many things.

It says in verses 2-3, "I know your deeds, your hard work and your perseverance. I know that you cannot tolerate wicked men, that you have tested those who claim to be apostles but are not, and have found them false. You have persevered and have endured hardships for My name, and have not grown weary. . . "

What a tremendous commendation! Even if you and I tried to measure up to this standard we would probably not earn the commendation given by Christ to the Ephesian church. But in spite of that, in verse 4 He says, "yet. . . I have something against you. You have forsaken your first love." He is not saying here - you do not love me. It is because of this church's love, that this church is doing all the things that are mentioned in verses 2-3. He is *not* saying you do not love me. But just loving Jesus is not enough. What He *is* saying in verse 4 is - not whether you love me but are you *in* love with me?

Jesus is not just expecting us to love Him in whatever way we can, but He is wanting from us that passionate, pre-eminent love of an undivided heart of devotion. He tells this church "you have forsaken that first love". He says, "remember the height from which you have fallen". He means that not loving Jesus with that first 'bridal kind of love' is sin.

Not loving Jesus with that kind of devotion that a bride has for her husband Jesus considers sin. Therefore in verse 5 He says, "Remember the height from which you have fallen! Repent and do the things you did at first." Then comes the terrible warning - "If you do not repent, I will come to you and remove your lampstand from its place."

We who are so full of works; we who are so zealous to work for the Lord; are in tremendous danger of forsaking that first love for Jesus. He is not asking here 'How good is your doctrine?' 'How long have you toiled?' He is not even asking: 'How much time are you spending at prayer meetings or studying the Word?' Just asking: 'Are you in love with me?'

This love for Jesus would mean that I do not refer to those kinds of things which are mechanical. When we get very busy, if you and I are honest, we admit that the first thing that gets knocked out is our prayer with God. We will not miss our meals very often. We try to make up whatever sleep we may have lost. But our prayer with our Lord does get left out. So we begin to offer Him our works instead of prayer. Yet the thing that He has been impressing upon me is God does not primarily want my works, He wants *me*. Not *what* I can offer Him. He is Sovereign, He is Almighty, with a word He can accomplish anything He wants. He really doesn't need you and me to bring people to Himself. But He does need us to be in that kind of a tremendous, beautiful, love relationship with Him.

And so the question we need to ask ourselves today is 'are we in love with Jesus?' Or, are we trying to offer up our works. In fact even prayer can become our works. We say 'I have spent so many hours in prayer' - 'I have fasted so many days' - 'I read so many chapters of the Bible' - 'I have visited so many homes' - 'I have preached in so many campaigns' - we have done so much! These things have become our works!

Let us remind ourselves that primarily He wants *us*, not so much our works. He wants our intimacy of walk with Him *before* we can offer works that are pleasing and delightful to Him. I think many of us are Christian workaholics. There is a tremendous danger of losing that intimacy and love for the Lord Jesus Christ. I am reminded of an evangelist who had a dream. This evangelist dreamt that he died and that he was standing at the Judgement Seat of Christ. As he approached the judgement of Christ, he was thinking: 'Now the Lord is going to commend me. I have conducted so many evangelistic campaigns. I have reached so many homes. I have sold thousands and thousands of pieces of literature.' Then God the Father appeared to him in his dream and looked down at him and said 'come closer my son, I want to see how much of my Son is in you'.

When, I believe, we stand in God's presence, His evaluation and judgement will be very different to ours. His purpose is to conform us to the image of His Son. All that we do, all that we learn, is so that we may be conformed to the image of God's Son. If, in all our working and in our labouring, and in all our praying we are not day by day, month by month, year by year conformed more and more into the image of His Son, we are failing somewhere very badly.

In 2 Cor 3:18 we read these words - "And we, who with unveiled faces all reflect the Lord's glory are being transformed into His likeness with ever-increasing glory, which comes from the Lord, who is the Spirit."

The test of God's life in me, of His pleasure in me even, is how much I am growing day by day in the likeness of His Son. When I come into this kind of heart communion with God, when I begin to look at Him, and He begins to change me into the likeness of His Son, some things happen. One, I change. Two, through prayer, God empowers me to change. Three, through prayer, God empowers me to change in love.

As I grow in my communion with God, in my walk with Him, I must change to be more like Jesus. Whenever I talk of this, I am reminded of an incident in my life when my children were quite small. You know, especially if you are mothers, that when the children are home during holidays they are always quarrelling with one another, pinching one another's things, pulling one another's hair. They are always calling out 'mama, she is doing this', and 'mama, she is doing that', you seem to be spending your time keeping peace between the two of them!

My son and daughter were no exception! They began quarrelling with one another at the beginning of the holiday and I thought, 'here goes my holiday' as I started making peace between them. The next morning when I was sat with my Bible, I encouraged my children to come and sit with me. I put my arms around them, as they joined me in prayer on my knees. I asked my son to turn to 1 Cor 13 and to read verses 4-7. Then I said:

"As you read these verses, instead of the word love put instead Jesus. Slowly he began to read:

"Jesus is patient, Jesus is kind, Jesus does not envy, Jesus does not boast, Jesus is not proud, He is not rude, He is not self seeking, He is not easily angered and He does not keep a record of wrongs" - and so on.

Then I said, "Peter, put your name and read." So he began to read:

"Peter is patient, Peter is kind. . ." Suddenly he burst out laughing.

I asked him, "Why are you laughing?"

He said, "But I am not patient. I am not kind."

Then I told him, "You have accepted the Lord Jesus into your heart, and the Lord Jesus is trying to make you like Himself, and if you say that from these verses this is how Jesus is, that must mean you must become like Jesus. You must be patient, and you must be kind and all the rest of it."

So we prayed together that God would make Peter more like Jesus and help him to be patient and kind and so on. He was so convicted by this, he went up to his room and took this motto, 'I must be patient, I must be kind'. He wrote the whole of these verses with his name in that holiday.

This is not only a word for children, but it is for all of us. We are to be conformed to Jesus Christ. We can test ourselves against this. Sometimes it is easy for us to be kind and patient to those outside our home, but we are so irritable, so impatient, so unkind to those who are in our home. This is another thing that we wives and mothers must face. Our homes are very important, and we have no business to be outside, what we make no effort to be in the home. My service and work outside the home, my ministry, is not really pleasing to the Lord unless I am able to show the same zeal in my home with my family. It is maintaining the vital breathing exercise of prayer which enables us to allow the life of Jesus to be expressed both inside and outside the home.

Chapter five

My personal experience

When I came first into women's work ten years ago, an Indian Christian leader was concerned, prayed with me and said these words. "You will not survive for more than three years - no woman leader has." But I thank God that I have been able to go on for ten years and am still going strong. The reason I believe is because I have two strong bases. Women are emotional beings, God has created us that way. We get emotionally battered and bruised very easily. We need a strong emotional support base without which we cannot function. I thank God today for the very strong emotional base I have in my family. Most especially for having prepared my husband in a wonderful way to accept this ministry God has given to me. I also thank God for the mission with whom I work - Operation Mobilisation. I have the privilege of being part of the India leadership team.

I have a very interesting marriage. I was brought up in Malaysia. My grandparents, my parents and I all lived there. I grew up to be quite an independent young woman. Then my marriage was arranged. I didn't see my husband until the day I married him. I don't know how that happened really - I wouldn't do it again. But I did. After my marriage I realised that he was a good orthodox South Indian husband!

He had very clear ideas of what a wife should be. So did I! I had very clear ideas of what a wife should be. But our ideas were not the same at all. He believed that a wife would just do and say what her husband wished her to do. She had no mind and no will of her own, she was there to submit. She was there for his convenience and his pleasure.

I knew that I was a real person. I had my own identity with a mind and will to think and to decide. You can guess what happened. For almost ten years of our marriage we had tremendous conflict. Because, I think, I fought for my own identity. I felt if I just submitted to him, said yes to everything he did, I would lose my very personhood, my respect for myself, my identity.

So I fought for this, and I tried every method. Nothing worked and as time went on things started to get very bad and my children, as they began to grow up, would see and question things. One day I took the Bible and read Ephesians 5 where it says 'wives submit to your husband in everything'. Then the Lord began to show me that it was not only what my husband was desiring, it was what my God, the Lord, desires of me. I began to argue with the Lord how unreasonable he was, how unjust he was, even He did not impose Himself into my life, He stood outside the door and knocked and allowed me to open the door to let Him enter in. Why should He give this right to my husband to rule me as he pleased. This argument continued for three years. I was a hard nut to crack!

But at the end of this time nothing had worked. Finally, I opened the Bible at Ephesians 5 and I said, 'Lord, I don't see any reason, any justice, any fairness in this world, because nothing has worked, but as this is what the Word says, I will obey'.

That morning I surrendered my will first to the Lord and then I surrendered my will to my husband. I changed overnight! Marriage relationships are grace relationships. I changed overnight by the grace of God. I submitted to everything he said, whatever it was, whether I liked it or not, whether I agreed with him or not. He was amazed because my life was so different. He couldn't understand what had happened.

He thought I was putting on a show and wondered what I was up to. Then he realised, as I was consistent, that I was really genuine, and something beautiful happened. God gave me back my faith and I learned a beautiful lesson. When God commands something, I can fight tooth and nail against it, but He knows best. If only I will release that will of mine, and say 'Lord, I will what you will', He takes it and does something beautiful.

For almost 13 years of my life I had struggled with all that I had for this freedom of mine and it never happened. I had heartache and tears, but at the end when I surrendered into God's hands, He gave it back to me in such a beautiful measure. In the old days when we had conflicts I used to pray 'Lord, change him', and nothing happened. I had to learn to pray 'Lord, change me; my pride, my stubbornness, my self-centredness'. As I began to deal with myself, God, in His gracious and beautiful way, began to deal with my husband.

So when I pray, when I am in this heart communion with God, then it is possible for me to change. His Spirit changes me, to conform me into the image of His Son, to be the kind of wife that I was not, but that God wanted me to be. He changed me by His grace.

We also find that this change is a grace relationship, only possible through the power of God. There are many prayers of Paul in the Bible but one of those that I have often prayed for myself and prayed for my friends is found in Colossians 1:9-14. Verse 11 reads:

". . . being strengthened with all power according to his glorious might so that you may have great endurance and patience, and joyfully giving thanks to the Father. . ."

This hand with which God strengthens me is with all power according to His glorious might. That is something beautiful that the Lord is teaching. I don't have the ability to do the things that God wants me to do. Even though I want to do them, often I cannot. That is what Paul also struggled with. In Romans 7:18-20 - "I know that nothing good lives in me, that is, in my sinful nature. For I have the desire to do what is good, but I cannot carry it out. For what I do is not the good I want to do; no, the evil I do not way to do - this I keep on doing. Now if I do what I do not want to do, it is no longer I who do it, but it is sin living in me that does it."

But here we are strengthened when we are in that communion with God - strengthened with all the power according to His glorious might - that means the unlimited power of God is available to you and to me. For what? Not to do mighty works, not to have huge campaigns, but so that we may have great endurance.

Living with someone who is totally different from you needs endurance. Getting along with someone who is difficult to get along with needs patience and endurance. To be able to do that, not gritting your teeth because you have no other way, but joyfully, needs power from on high. So it was it my relationships in those days. As I changed, I came to an understanding with my husband as we are almost totally opposite in temperament.

I like people, I like talking to people, like entertaining people. But he is a man of very, very few words. So when any visitors come, he will hardly talk. Not that he doesn't like them, but he just doesn't talk. So when I go to make tea, there he sits twiddling his thumbs uttering not a word. There my visitors sit, shuffling around, not knowing what to do. I used to get very embarrassed!

Afterwards I would say to him, 'why don't you talk to them?' He would say, 'but what am I to talk about?' So we would get into arguments! Another difference between us is that I am one who likes to see everything in its proper place. My husband is different. He would read his newspaper and one piece would be dropped in the drawing room, another piece in the dining room, another in the bedroom or in the bathroom! I like my cupboard doors to be closed - he opens the cupboard doors and doesn't close them. I like my floors to be clean - but he is a research scientist. He walks home probably thinking incredibly lofty thoughts. He doesn't notice where he is walking, and so he will come into the house all mucky and dirty and just walk on my clean floors, not even realising that he is dirtying my floors. How do I react?

Let me tell you. One evening my dear husband rushes in from work very excited, as he has something important he wants to tell me. But it has been raining and is very muddy outside. Does my husband notice that? He doesn't! He rushes in trampling his mud and dirt onto my bright shiny clean red floor. I don't look at his face. I don't even see that he has something to tell me. I look at the muddy prints on my floor, and I lose my temper with him. "Why didn't you wipe your feet outside on the mat," I yelled at him. That starts a big argument. Each accusing the other of what really are petty things.

The Lord began to teach me something. Things didn't get any better. My husband didn't change. So the Lord taught me one important principle. People matter more than things. We are called to love people and use things. So often we use people and love things.

The Lord taught me it was pointless, worthless, useless, and profitless to pick an argument and lose my relationship and peace with my husband, just because some things are out of place and other things are dirty. There are the situations in which we need endurance and patience in order to lead a joyful life.

Take, for example, toothpaste. You all know there are two ways of squeezing a tube of toothpaste. One way you squeeze it from the bottom up neatly. The other way is just to squeeze anywhere. As you can guess, I do it the correct way - from the bottom up. Edison, my husband, does it the other way. So whenever I get it all straightened out, and the next day the neatness is spoiled, I get irritated. The third day I blow up - over toothpaste! We lose our peace with one another. My husband and I have even quarrelled over the toilet paper! Which way the roll should hang! Little things irritate us. We need patience and endurance as we live with one another. I think the family is the ground that God has given to us to refine us in order that He can see us conformed to His Son. So we learn that we cannot change ourselves, it is God who empowers us to change.

In Ephesians 4:30 we read - "And do not grieve the Holy Spirit of God, with whom you were sealed for the day of redemption." That leads directly into verses 31 and 32 - "Get rid of all bitterness, rage and anger, brawling and slander, along with every form of malice. Be kind and compassionate to one another, forgiving each other, just as in Christ God forgave you."

I want to ask you as I ask myself - am I so in communion with God that my priorities and my perspectives are as God desires. Or have I, with my work and my zeal and my programmes and my statistics and my reports, got everything upside down, so that the things outside seem to be more important than the things at home. Are my external actions and words more important to me than what goes on inside?

I believe there are many who will read this who are hurting inside. There was a Sunday school which I was asked to supervise. That is to just go and observe. In this particular class the teacher was teaching on forgiveness, from Luke 17:3-4 and Matthew 18:21-22 where Jesus told Peter to forgive "70 times 7". It was a beautiful lesson. The teacher gave her own testimony. Then I asked permission to say a few words to the children (10-12 years old). I said, "you have heard this lesson on forgiveness, how many of you are not speaking to someone else in school? How many of you are angry with somebody else?" You know, every little hand went up.

This is just as relevant for you and I. If you believe in the Word of God, this is what Jesus Christ expects of you and me, forgiveness is an area in which God has to teach us lessons again and again. If you do not forgive others, God will not forgive you. Remember the Lord's prayer 'Our Father, forgive us our sins as we forgive others'. This means I am telling God I cannot forgive this person, so you don't forgive me. How can we do without the forgiveness of God? As Ephesians 4:32 says - "be kind and compassionate to one another, forgiving each other, just as in Christ God forgave you".

Now sometimes, somebody does something wrong and we forgive them the first time. They do a second wrong and we forgive them. The third time you get angry with them. How many times must I forgive them?

If God were to ask that question of me and you, what would happen to us? How many times again and again do we go to God asking for forgiveness? Does He push us away? We are told just as He forgives us, we are to forgive. We are to practice this lesson of forgiveness with the family, i.e. husbands and wives, parents and children, brothers and sisters. In this community of Jesus' people the words of Jesus in John 13:34 are the perfect example of how we should live. "A new command I give you: Love one another. As I have loved you, so you must love one another."

Not by our preaching, not by activities, but by the love we can have for one another, which cannot be of the world, but can only be of God. By this love shall all men know we are His disciples.

In relationships we find that some of us are like the

'touch me not' plant. Have you seen a 'touch me not' plant? It is a small plant but if you touch it, it just curls up. It just closes up tight. We are often like that - we just close up. We don't talk any more, because we are upset, or angry, or hurt. There are the other people who, when they get angry and upset, are like porcupines. You know what a porcupine is? It shoots quills. Porcupines hit out. When we quarrel, as husbands and wives, or with colleagues, we can be like either of the two. Sulk and go silent, or hit out. So we go into cold war or hot war. Let me give you an illustration about a silent couple. They hadn't been talking to one another for three weeks. But habits die hard. They always went for a drive each evening. This particular evening they were driving but not speaking when by the roadside they saw some donkeys. The husband looked at his wife and for the first time in three weeks spoke to her. "Some of your relatives?" To which the wife promptly retorted, "Yes, on my husband's side".

So quick to hurt one another. So slow to be reconciled to one another. The ministry of reconciliation must start in the home. I remember the time when the Lord taught this lesson concerning my husband. It was a night when we had a big argument. Those were the days before I submitted my will to God and to my husband. I wanted to get involved in some campaign in the church, and my husband refused to agree. We had an argument and went to bed, very angry with one another, though the Bible tells us don't go to bed when you are angry.

The next morning, I got up and sat with the Word. The Lord began to convict me of my pride. I argued with God.

I said 'this is your work, I am doing something good.' He said 'Pride, go and ask your husband's forgiveness.'

I argued that there was nothing wrong in what I had done so why should I go and ask his forgiveness? He should come and ask my forgiveness, for the argument, and for his pig headedness and his stubbornness in not allowing me to do this thing.

But there the voice of the Spirit said, 'ask forgiveness. Even though you are 90% right, you are still 10% wrong, because you got angry and you argued. So for the 10% wrong, go and say you are sorry'.

Now I learned that in a quarrel, sometimes we are sorry, we are ready to be reconciled, but we are waiting for the other person to come and take the first step. As God's children, God is telling us that in any quarrel there is a part that each one has in that quarrel. It may not be a major part but still it is a part. For that go and say sorry. These are words that are very hard to say. Sometimes we will do everything to show we are sorry, but we don't want to say the word, 'sorry'.

That morning, as I sat, I was convicted of my pride. I was convicted to go and ask my husband's forgiveness. Inside me, everything rebelled, but finally I submitted to the Lord.

Now when my husband is kind to me, I put out his shirt and pants, I give him his coffee in bed, and make a hot breakfast for him. I do all the things that a good Indian wife does. But when my husband is unkind to me, I let him take care of himself. I don't do any of those things. For a few weeks, I had been quite sore at him and so he had been looking after himself.

So here I was this morning, the Spirit of God convicting me. I took his coffee to bed. I took out his pants and shirt and his clothes. I would do everything except to let the words escape from my lips. To say I am sorry, forgive me, just wouldn't come. In my heart I kept praying, 'Lord, help me to say these words, help me to be reconciled, because that is pride not being able to bow down, to bend, to humble myself. Finally, just before he left, I said 'I am sorry, forgive me for my quarrel last night, and I will listen to what you have to say.'

He is a man of few words. He never said anything. He went off to his work and I began to stew inside again. I thought that at least he could have said 'It's alright'. Even if he didn't want to say he was sorry. Then he has gone without a word. I took that back to the Lord and said, "Lord, just handle this. I am free in my heart and I have forgiven." The Lord has his own ways. My husband went to his office, but couldn't get the thought of me out of his head. He had been impressed that I had not argued, I had not quarrelled, I had not talked back to him. I had been, as the Bible says, kind and compassionate, tender hearted and forgiving.

And so he came back home. He virtually never comes back home once he's left for his office. He's the kind of man who gets totally absorbed in his work. But that day he came back and he said, "I'm sorry, forgive me." This was the first time in his life he had ever said 'I'm sorry' to me. He then told me I could get involved in the campaign at church. God's ways are truly beyond our ways, and God has His priorities. God's priority is building a community of people, not so much to do His work, which is also there, but first and primarily, a community of God's people exhibiting in themselves and reflecting through their lives, individually and corporately in the family, in their fellowship, in their organisation, the life and beautiful character of the God to whom we belong.

Chapter six

Women's role in evangelism

Religious thinking and teaching often shape a person's values and estimates of worth. For instance, a Jewish man might think: "Lord, I thank you that I am not a Gentile, a slave or a woman".

A traditional Hindu would believe that a person cannot attain salvation as a woman except through being reborn as a man. This is her Karma. They would also believe that a woman is irresponsible: so in childhood she obeys her father, in youth her husband and in old age her son.

In the Koran, "men have authority over women because Allah has made the one superior to the other. . . as for those from whom you fear disobedience, admonish them, beat them".

Christianity teaches that a woman, like a man, is created in the image of God. She is redeemed in Christ to be "joint-heirs" of the grace of life. There is no male or female before God.

In the 19th century the church pioneered the education of women. They were trained as doctors and nurses to treat other women. Though the church pioneered these reforms in society, it has never fully opened its own doors to women. Jane Hatfield's research revealed the following:

"Women missionaries in India who were competent and financially independent were not replaced by

Indian women, because women's ministry was not held in high respect. So parents discouraged their daughters from entering a career which would make them a less desirable match in marriage. Furthermore, the churches prefer to train men whom congregations would readily accept.

"The churches became preoccupied trying to establish their position in the Indian society after the colonial rule. Women's work was thus relegated often to avoid antagonism."

The encouragement of women in ministry still faces similar struggles today. We cannot talk of 'evangelising' women till the Christian women are themselves built up to understand their role and be aware of their responsibilities.

In 1982, I co-ordinated the work among women for an evangelistic campaign called "Bangalore Penetration". Though I'd lived in Bangalore since 1962, I had never been made aware of the needs of many of the women. For the first time I walked into a slum, half a kilometre from my home. I was shocked at what I saw. Since then the Spirit of God has compelled me into working among these women. I was a teacher and happy in my work and ministry among students. For one long year I struggled. Evelyn Christenson, whose Prayer Seminars I co-ordinated in India, put her hand on my shoulder one day and commissioned me to women's work. I was staggered but yielded to God's will.

Because of our Indian culture it is very difficult for women to be in leadership positions in evangelical circles. For most of us it is a lonely struggle. In 1987 I resigned from Evangelical Fellowship of India (EFI). Recognising God had called me into Indian women's ministry, Operation Mobilisation (OM) offered their umbrella under which I have worked since 1988. I value greatly their strong prayer base and the warm encouragement from brothers and sisters of the OM family both in India and overseas!

I long to see Indian women free from their shackles and chains, blossoming forth in the beauty and maturity for which they have been created! I labour and toil to this end.

Of course the status of the Indian woman has gone through a continuous process of change. But through it all runs the dominating thread of her 'low self-image' imposed upon her by family, church and society from the time of her birth till her death.

Boys are still preferred to girls in many countries of the world. In 1986, a report appeared in *India Today* that shocked its readers. It was about the practice of killing girl babies that is still prevalent in some communities and becoming increasingly widespread today. A girl is often considered a liability.

Tradition clothes the husband with a 'god-image'. In many places, the new bride prostrates herself at her husband's feet on the threshold of her new home. This symbolises her servitude to him all her life. No matter how she is treated in her husband's home, normally she can no longer go back to her parents. There is an Indian proverb that says, "Woman is like spit; once spat out she cannot be taken back". Unfortunately, many believe this!

One magazine described women as 'the poorest of the

poor, oppressed of the oppressed'. One Christian leader maintained that 'the largest untouched people-group in India is women'!

Due to this oppression, exploitation and suppression, the Joint Women's Organisations have begun to voice their anger with violent protest against these injustices and inequalities. Only the feminist activist's voice is heard. Though these Joint Women's Organisations have done laudable work, they have in the process pitted woman against her God as well as man. Conversely, the evangelical female voice is almost non-existent in Asian society. Women need to be told, and also to hear in loud and clear tones that they can reach their full potential IN CHRIST. Then they must act according to that knowledge.

Her low self-image gives her a deep sense of inadequacy and helplessness. She is full of fear and is a victim of her own prejudices. She is a silent sufferer.

Vicky is a somewhat typical young woman. This is how she thinks:

> "Untold millions are still untold, untold millions are outside the fold. Lord I'm aware of your concern for these millions, here am I, but send my brother.
>
> "I love the Lord and so want to please Him. But I'm only a woman and I can't even look at a harmless little lizard, never mind a snake! How can I go far away, 'in heathen darkness dwelling', to tell the millions who forever may be lost, unless someone tells them salvation's story. . ."

She continues with her thinking -

> "Even if I did go, no one would listen to us women in this land. It is our culture. Some say women are

meant for the kitchen only. No one will believe or accept what a woman says."

Yet, did not God use many women even in our country to fulfil His purposes? Will not this challenge us to GO? All we need is to obey and trust the Lord to enable us.

There are countless testimonies where women who have come to know the Lord have led whole families to Him. By keeping an open home, a woman can share her faith with all who enter. The broken and helpless can be brought in to find physical and emotional healing and peace through Jesus Christ.

Large numbers of prayer groups are run by women in Madras. It is reported that housewives in the localities come and many of them are converted.

Would I trust God and obey in spite of all the fears welling within me? Again the excuse of my womanhood stood strongly before me. 'It's a risk Lord'. But the Lord encouraged me from 1 Corinthians 16:9 - "because a great door for effective work has opened to me, and there are many who oppose me."

The 'Manila Manifesto' further states that "*We deeply regret that many of our congregations are inward-looking, organised for maintenance rather than mission, or pre-occupied with church-based activities at the expense of witness*".

It is profoundly disturbing to face the possibility that over a long period of time the church may have been denying to women the place assigned to them by God. But there is no growth without pain and struggle and in this area as in others, the church must come to maturity.

If it is true that "the church is God's agent in the earth -

the medium through which He expresses Himself to the world." Could we then seriously ask ourselves whether the reason God has not been able to fully express Himself to the world, the reason the church is not marching forward in Christ's mission in the world, is because she is not a fully functioning church? She is handicapped and crippled, particularly because the tremendous potential and possibilities of women have not been developed.

A. The Biblical role

The "Manila Manifesto" states that *"God created men and women as equal bearers of his image (Gen 1:26-27), accepts them equally in Christ (Gal 3:28) and poured out his Spirit on all flesh, sons and daughters alike (Acts 2:17-18). In addition, because the Holy Spirit distributes His gifts to women as well as to men, they must be given opportunities to exercise their gifts. We celebrate their distinguished record in the history of missions and are convinced that God calls women to similar roles today. Even though we are not fully agreed what forms their leadership should take, we do agree about the partnership in world evangelisation which God intends men and women to enjoy. Suitable training must therefore be made available to both."*

B. Resistance from culture and society

The low place of women, who are treated more as vessels to be used and exploited rather than persons to be loved and developed, is not only a Third World phenomenon.

Women need to be assured again and again of their

identity in CHRIST. In spite of their cultural inhibitions and natural timidity, they need to be taught and trained to take up their responsibilities and encouraged to develop their God-given gifts for the building up of the family, the church and in the extension of His Kingdom. This is what Operation Mobilisation India, through its ARPANA ministries, is seeking to do across the country through conferences, family life seminars, prayer seminars, training programmes and through different workshops. In many places this is a new emphasis, an exciting and indeed liberating message for women. They are excited, totally open and show deep hunger for the things of God.

Through these ministries, women's leadership has been developed. Families are being reconciled and enriched. Women's gifts for service are released and developed and needy women are being reaching with the gospel.

Now a network of women for the purpose of encouraging and spurring one another to good works is springing up. Specific ministries are also being developed among women. . . prayer, Bible study, slum ministry, that is both gospel outreach and practical help to the poorest of the poor. Surely every Christian woman needs to be involved in these three areas. However, materials for teaching and training purposes written by local women for their own context to meet their particular needs is essential. Unfortunately most of the best training materials for women seem to come from the USA. If it is good, it's good in an American context. There is a desperate need for material written by Indian women for an Indian context, Thai women for a Thai context, etc.

There is a new awakening among women. It is exciting

as it were, 'to see them emerging from their cocoons'!
Social activism left in its wake an emptiness creating
within a deep need for deeper experience of God and
hunger for His Word. A spirit of prayer has gripped our
people. God is moving in pockets of people here and
there. Is there a new heart that God is putting into us
women? We have passed from despair and hopelessness
to yearning and longing and I believe we are now entering
yet another phase - that of expectation. And who can
indeed estimate what God can do through women whose
hearts are burdened for a broken world, filled with God's
love and empowered by the Holy Spirit to communicate
the love of Christ?

1. Special centres of study and training for women to be set up

Particularly we need to think of the study of feminine
perspectives, insights and understanding of women's
needs in family and society

2. Our individual gifts to be harnessed and strengthened. Then released to develop special women's ministries:

What are some of these gifts? Servanthood - one of the
hardest things.

sick visiting	-	both in hospitals and homes
mentally disturbed	-	finding and ministering to
hospitality	-	open home, idal opportunities for evangelism
aged	-	thinking of better ways to care

prayer	-	real genuine prayer
prisoners	-	some are in atrocious conditions
counselling	-	but make sure you get some training
prostitutes	-	how many dare to try and help these fallen ones
Bible study	-	so many want to learn more
women living in slums	-	many in appaling conditions
giving	-	some can have a biblical ministry of financial giving

3. The Church should be the base for mobilising women

a. **Recognition** - the God given gifts, talents, and abilities of women should be recognised by the church, so that the women can be involved in various aspects of the ministry to a much greater measure than occurs at present.

b. **Teaching and training** - Adequate materials giving the biblical teaching on women's ministry should be provided, if necessary, by compiling existing materials and writing of additional materials.

c. **Encouragement to serve** - The local churches should motivate and encourage Christian women to work in a holistic ministry using bridges like the following:

Christian festivals

Sewing and cooking classes

Adult literacy classes

Hospital visitation
Neighbourhood children's work
Neighbourhood Bible studies

Rejected and neglected groups, such as prostitutes and prisoners, should be a vital target for evangelism.

4. Christian homes to become centres of caring and nurture of new converts and rehabilitated persons.

When young Hindu, Muslim or totally unchurched women become Christians, they often receive no nurture. Hence, they can easily slip back into the religious and cultural customs of their homes. Christian homes in their own community should be sought out for the purpose of spiritual nurture and establishment.

5. Ministry of friendship

The ministry of friendship, especially amongst our so called "middle classes" means infinite expenditure of time, sympathy and love to place ourselves alongside these women, to enter into their lives, to share their aspirations It means willingness also to lay ourselves open to not a few snubs and repulses. In many ways it is harder than contact with the poorer classes, who often quickly and gratefully respond, and do not so speedily pull us up by their hot resentment the instant we show the cloven hoof of our fancied superiority and behave as if we had come to 'work among them' rather than to love them and seek their friendship.

A young medical doctor felt led to open a clinic in a

predominately Muslim area with the help of her husband. Very soon she found the Muslim women coming to her in large numbers. What was the reason? Was it because they could not go to men doctors? That was, of course, an important reason. But there was another. Word spread around that this lady doctor listened to them as they poured out their hearts to her. She loved them and expressed her understanding and concern for them. So they came. In many cultures today only women can reach women.

6. Men and women co-ordinatin together

The men's and women's work should be closely co-ordinated, so that whenever a woman is under instruction her husband may be fished for by one of the men missionaries, and vice versa. That whole families may be won for Christ and, wherever possible, the terrible divisions and breaking up of homes may be averted. At present in India we see not infrequently whole districts in which there are only women missionaries and again other districts in which only men are working, and the result is a terrible hindering of the progress of the gospel.

7. Literature

One of the great obstacles to change lies in the women. It is the women who are moulding their baby sons and daughters in Hindu mythology today. It is the influence of wife and mother that holds back many a secret convert from confession. It is the women, who can be a powerful factor in the upheaval to liberty when it comes. How can these women be reached? There is an ever increasing body of women who can read and who can be influenced in their homes, if only we have the right literature to give them. This is equally true of other cultures.

8. Culture

In India, which is predominantly Hindu, the mother's influence over the children, both boys and girls, up to about ten years of age, is paramount. Women are the conservative element in the defence of their faith. We ought to lay far more emphasis on work among Hindu women as a means for hastening the evangelism for Indians. There needs to be an understanding of the customs and culture that rule their behaviour and thinking patterns. Only then can the gospel be made relevant to them.

9. Caste

One of the greatest cultural barriers to the gospel in modern history has been the caste system - a powerful institution in India that has frustrated the work of missionaries for centuries. Much of India is still deeply enmeshed in the caste system. How to approach the caste system, therefore, continues to be a knotty issue. One of the most significant missiological studies to appear on the subject in recent years has come from the pen of BV Subbamma, a caste-Hindu whose own pilgrimage to Christianity was hindered by caste.

Subbamma was introduced to Christianity as a child while attending a Lutheran mission school in South India.

She initially resisted biblical teachings, believing Christianity was a religion of the Harijans (outcasts). Eventually, however, after reading the Bible for herself, her life was transformed. "The name of Jesus became so precious to me that I could hardly believe it. . . I was supremely happy, having the assurance that Jesus Christ had suffered for my sin and had forgiven me and blessed me with salvation." A major obstacle, however, loomed before her: "The question of baptism disturbed me. I was definitely not prepared to leave my own Kamma people and join some other community. At the same time, I longed to be baptised since I understood one had to be baptised if she wished to be a disciple of the Lord." After enduring considerable personal turmoil and opposition from her family, Subbamma was baptised and paid the tremendous price of complete identification with the existing church made up of Harijan Christians.

10. The outcast

Poor and illiterate

These are often the untouchables amongst whom even the Christian women are reluctant to minister. Women in Bombay will spend Rs.100 a day on a slimming clinic whereas the Adivasi women in Orissa would sell their babies for Rs.100 in order to survive.

On average, 70% of these women are illiterate, 65% under-nourished, and 45% are below poverty level. Women must be involved in meeting these needs through adult literacy classes, income generating schemes and employment skills.

Prostitutes

There is a social stigma on prostitutes. Fear of this rubbing onto them prevents many Christians from having anything to do with them. Dr I S Gilada, the Honorary President of the Indian Health Organisation, reported that there are over 300,000 prostitutes in the metropolitan cities of Bombay, Delhi, Calcutta, Pune and Nagpur. Poverty and unemployment are some of the causes.

It has been reported that 25% of the women in the red light areas of Bombay have been abducted and sold; 8% have been sold by their fathers after being forced into incestuous relationships. Nearly 6% have been raped and sold later while 15% had been dedicated to the Goddess Yellamma. The Yellamma system in Karnataka alone annually sends around 8,000 girls to the brothels in Pune and Bombay. Almost 150,000 prostitutes in Bombay and Pune constitute the single largest profession for working women in the city. In Pune, 15-20% of the women have been sold to prostitution by their husbands. Morally they have lost everything - even their self-respect.

However good a government rehabilitation programme may be for these prostitutes, having been removed from the brothels and brought into rehabilitation centres, they still feel degraded and unclean. Only Christ can offer forgiveness and cleansing so that they can be transformed new persons to start life afresh.

11. Conclusion

Pray that with undaunting courage, spurred by our immense confidence in our God and our intense love for our people, we Christian women will help to set aside prejudices, break down barriers, rise above pressures in order that we may go forth to touch others for Christ. Lord restore unto us our sense of worth, the dignity of our womanhood!

Pray that God may raise many women in our land who would, like Esther, be willing to be instruments of purpose in God's hands - cleansed and available for use. Who will have the commitment of Esther and say as she did - "Go, gather together all the Jews who are in Susa, and fast for me. Do not eat or drink for three days, night or day. I and my maids will fast as you do. When this is done, I will go to the king, even though it is against the law. And if I perish, I perish." Esther 4:16

Chapter seven

A call to action

The scope for women in missions

As I have attempted to study the subject in order to write this book, I have been bewildered to find myself in a sort of 'theological wonderland' where *words* have so many meanings.

The two fictitious characters, Alice and Humpty Dumpty, were having a conversation:

"When I use a word", Humpty Dumpty said in rather a scornful tone, "it means just what I choose it to mean, nothing more or less."

"The question is", said Alice, "whether you can make words mean different things."

"The question is", said Humpty Dumpty, "which is the master - that's all."

The issue - *can MEN manipulate the meaning of words* - is still a contemporary one. Dr John Stott in his paper at the Deolali Congress mentions that, especially in the past two decades, humorous Humpty Dumptys have enjoyed playing with words. Here it would be with words like: 'woman', her 'status/role', 'mission'. It is not the purpose of this book to enter into this controversy about their meanings and interpretations, but to put forth the challenge of all that women *can* do and *should* do under God in mission. It is also a plea to pastors, leaders and husbands to encourage the development of this potential for God's glory. With much prayerful consideration therefore I have sought the guidance of the Holy Spirit to present to you my deep conviction of what the 'Role of Women in Mission' is.

The pattern set by Jesus

Opinions vary concerning the interpretation of the attitude of our Lord towards women, His acceptance and expectation of them, as shown in the Gospels. However, "all the Synoptic accounts stress the importance of women in the passion and resurrection narratives. It is as though Luke especially wanted to highlight the place of women in the mission of the Messiah", says Donald Gutherie in his book New Testament Theology.

Jesus treated women as they should be treated. He never treated them as 'the women, God help us!' or 'the ladies, God bless them'. He rebuked without querulousness and praised without condescension. He took their questions and arguments seriously. He never mapped out their sphere for them.

Is it any wonder that, although all the apostles appointed by Jesus were men, the band of supporters who went with Jesus included women. Some of them had been delivered from evil spirits and infirmities, but all of them provided financial backing for the mission (Luke 8:1-3). Not all these women were young for Mary, the mother of James and Joseph, and the mother of the sons of Zebedee are both mentioned. These women were willing to allow their children to leave their jobs and homes and follow

Jesus. How rare it is today for mothers to relinquish their children for the mission of Jesus! "For whoever does the will of my Father in heaven is my brother and sister and mother." (Matt 12:50, Mark 3:35, Luke 8:21)

Jesus taught women about Himself, e.g. Mary and Martha at Bethany. The Rabbi's denied the need for teaching women God's law, and today that sentiment still largely exists. A corollary of knowing the Lord is witnessing to Him, as did Mary Magdelene and the Samaritan woman. From the example of Jesus we see that women need to be taught the Bible so that they can become effective witnesses for Him. What urgent emphasis, what priority is there to give quality teaching and training for women in our agenda? It is further noteworthy that Jesus revealed the wonder of His resurrection reality first to Mary Magdelene - and that she became the first evangelist when Jesus gave her the responsibility and privilege to "go and tell".

The programme of the Early Church

Mary, the mother of John Mark, opened her house for prayer (Acts 12:12). Women were also in the upper room praying when the Holy Spirit came upon the disciples and women spoke in tongues at Pentecost (Acts 1:14; 2:17-18). Both men and women believed in Christ, were baptised and were persecuted (Acts 5:14; 8:12; 9:2; 17:4, 12). According to the Jews, women did not come as part of the quota needed to have a Synagogue; but in contrast, Luke consistently noted in Acts that women were also involved in the growth of the church.

Lydia, the business woman, when she opened her heart to the Lord, shared the Good News with her own household. Though she must have been a busy woman she offered practical hospitality even risking her own reputation by opening her home to the ex-prisoners Paul and Silas (Acts 16:13ff).

Tabitha is described as being full of good works and charity (Acts 9:36). Philip's four daughters were prophetesses (Acts 21:8). Priscilla as well as Aquila explained the way of God more accurately to Apollos (Acts 18:26). It is worthy to note that she travelled willingly with her husband, moving from place to place. It is a wonderful ability, especially in a woman, to pull up roots and be willing to go to a place that is alien because of the greater need of the gospel there.

Paul greets many women in Romans 16. Phoebe is called 'deacon' (servant); Priscilla and Aquila are fellow workers; Mary worked hard among the congregation. It is clear that women participated in the spread of the gospel and their role was not entirely limited to non-verbal help (Priscilla taught).

A woman's role is therefore not just in the background, while her husband gets more involved. Every woman should be active in witnessing for Christ in one way or another. Paul Tournier says, "He calls us to an adventure of faith difficult and exciting but full of poetry, of new discoveries, of fresh turns and sudden surprises." No power on earth indeed can deter the mighty advance of the gospel when the Holy Spirit is permitted to equip and empower His people, both men and women, for evangelism.

"The Lord gives the word (of power); the women
who hear publish (the news) are a great host."

(Ps 68:11 Amplified)

Then why are some of us (women) so hidden? Our
"hiddenness" comes from the desire to 'play it safe'.
Never to take any risks. Never to make a fresh commitment to trust in God. We look at our own resources and
say 'I could never do that'! "Our sacred littleness keeps us
in a box", says Charles Swindoll.

The analogy of the church as the Body of Christ

The New Testament regards the church as the Body of
Christ. Grasp this precious and beautiful idea and we
begin to see that every Christian has a part to play in the
church and a very important part. 1 Cor 12 speaks of the
most diverse parts in the Body of Christ working together
in one smooth-running body. There is thus harmony and
beauty when every single part operates properly. Where is
efficiency and effectiveness, there is growth. Varieties of
gifts are spoken of in 1 Cor 12:4. More than half the
Body is women. Would to God every Christian woman be
taught to become aware of her God-given gifts and learn to
develop them! "Unused gifts waste the grace of God and
choke spiritual life both personally and corporately", says
Pamela Heim. By gifts I don't mean spectacular gifts like
healing, miracles, prophecy, tongues, interpretation but
also those like prayer, giving, mercy, hospitality and faith.
Malvin Hodges states that "the church is God's agent on
the earth - the medium through which He expresses Himself to the world". Could we then seriously ask ourselves

whether the reason God has not been able to fully express Himself to the world, the reason the church is not marching forward in Christ's mission in the world, is because the tremendous potential and possibilities of women have not been developed?

Miriam Noff in her article *Why I Question the Feminist Movement* says,

> "God is an economist. He desires that I operate at full capacity with every gift He gives and with every ounce of His empowering energy. But we've internalised the worldly view that *top* is best."

Miriam means that service should embrace a hundred and more things a woman can do in a church. So why this struggle for the position of pastor or teacher alone? Is it because with the world, the church also believes that the key to having status is to be the leader? How did Jesus lead His disciples? He washed their feet, walked by their side and served them. Jesus said, "Instead, whoever wants to become great among you must be your servant, and whoever wants to be first must be your slave - just as the Son of Man did not come to be served, but to serve, and to give his life as a ransom for many." (Matt 20:24-28) This then is the secret of Christian ministry. Not self-exaltation but Christ's glory: not self-glory but sacrifice. With the varied gifts God has given me, I can serve best as the woman He created.

Why? I believe that the first major obstacle lies in the church's attitude and values regarding women. 49% of India's population is women. Our national leaders clearly understood the importance of the role of women and the tremendous potential in Indian women, which needed to be harnessed for the building of a new India.

Mahatma Gandhi, the "father" of the Indian nation, used to say that to teach the entire family, the woman of the family must first be taught.

Pandit Nehru, the first Indian Prime Minister, once said, "To awaken the people it is the woman who must be awakened. Once she is on the move the family moves, the village moves, the nation moves". Hence, it is obvious that unless this vast reservoir of women is adequately tapped and effectively released, one cannot expect to make rapid changes for the building up of the church and the extension of God's kingdom.

The second equally major obstacle is the self-oppression of women themselves who do not seriously believe God is willing to penetrate the inner springs of their character and begin a solitary revolution there. They do not believe that God can and needs to work through the likes of them. This is because of the low self image ingrained into us by our society and culture. But who can know what God can do through women whose hearts are burdened for a broken world, filled with God's love and empowered with the Holy Spirit to communicate the love of Christ? Who can estimate what the church and the Kingdom of God owe to dedicated womenfolk? And it is women who can reach women more effectively and successfully than anyone else in our culture.

Beloved sisters, "The harvest is past, the summer has ended, and we are not saved." (Jeremiah 8:20). Does that mean anything to you? Are you willing to reconstruct your life in such a way that you will be a smooth flowing river whose banks channel you to the things of eternal significance? But are you clean today? I can't talk to you about missions if there is guilt in your heart because of unconfessed sin or because you doubt God's grace. J T Scamonds says, "Christian missions is the biggest business because it gives the greatest dividend". But are you willing enough and concerned enough to be involved and to pay the price?

The history of women in missions

When women are given the freedom to serve the Lord and use the gifts God has given them, what actually happens in practice? Does a monstrous regiment of women take over and dominate? Let's turn back the pages of history to learn what lessons God would teach us through them.

We know that the 19th century church in India pioneered the education of women and the training of women to be doctors and nurses to treat women. But though she pioneered these reforms in society, the church herself never fully opened her own doors to women in the years of 'mission' before independence in 1947. Jane Hatfield researched the reasons for this:

First she suggests that women missionaries who were competent and financially independent were not replaced by Indian women because women's ministry was not held in high respect. So parents discouraged their daughters from entering a career which would make them a less desirable match in marriage. Furthermore, with the decreasing finances, the churches preferred to train men whom congregations would readily accept.

Second, the churches became pre-occupied in trying

to establish their position in the Indian society after the colonial rule. Third, the cultural attitudes toward women have dominated the church more than Biblical attitudes.

The Indian church needs to recover her heritage. The women in India, in spite of their cultural inhibition and natural timidity, need to be enabled to function fully and effectively within the Body of Christ. Would it be far-fetched to say that the key to the evangelisation of India is the women?

God has given women a tremendous capacity for love, understanding and work. There are a great number of godly women who can help pastors turn the tide of broken homes that is sweeping into our churches. They can also teach women the Bible so that women will stand firm on the truth, in the midst of false teaching that assails the churches. They need to be awakened to their responsibilities and encouraged to develop and use their God-given gifts in the Body. Several problems can be worked out as women learn from women how to cope with life. Thus they learn to be better women, better citizens of their country.

Women's involvement today

We're living in a fog. Black and white have become grey. Church leaders are lost in the mist. Time is running out! The ugly street violence sends a chill through the whole nation. The very fabric of our society is torn apart and long cherished ideals and values are trampled under-foot in the streets of our cities. Accepted norms of behaviour are being swept away; there is confusion in every area of life, where the very foundations of our society are subjects for debate and question. No-one has an answer. The moral slide in every area shocks us.

Christians must get out into the world and permeate and infiltrate it. But when they get all mixed up with liberalism, secularism and socialism then the influence is diluted and the salt loses its savour. So there is a right involvement and a wrong involvement. A right way to identify with society and a wrong way. 'In the world but not of the world', said Jesus. It is true, we ought to make conditions as favourable as we possibly can. As Vance Havner aptly put it, "When we get on the band- wagon with political reformers trying to bring in our own millennium by education, legislation, sanitation, ventilation and every other action, we are out of context and we get so occupied with doing this old world over, that we forget our other worldliness and our unworldliness and our next worldliness. The whole business can be perverted by the devil until we end up helping to build up old Babylon down here instead of looking for the new Jerusalem." But this, however, is no excuse for the majority of Christians to live as if they had cotton wool in their ears and blindfolds around their eyes trying to pretend nothing has happened! Is this why, for so long, the secular humanistic feminist voice has been the only voice heard in India? Though it has done laudable work in the last two decades to uplift women, in the process it has pitted the women against her God and against men. The Indian evangelical female voice is almost non-existent in the society. Women need to hear again, in loud and ear tones, and know that they can reach their full potential in Christ.

Examples from Scripture

Vast numbers of women are listed in God's Honour Roll and the glories of many more are unnamed and unsung. We have already looked into some examples in the New Testament. Let us look in some detail at only two from the Old Testament. I have selected the following for their parallel relevance to us today.

Esther

Even though Queen Esther, the only Jewess in the palace, was very limited in what she could do, the point is she did what she could. She did not just sit back and blame her circumstances. She knew she should shine for the Lord Jehovah, even in the palace, and that's what she did. Who knows, you too may 'have come to the Kingdom for a time such as this'. God has put you where you are to be salt, to be a witness. She did not let her fears overcome her. She prepared herself with prayer and fasting. With undauntable courage, spurred by her immense confidence in her God and her intense love of her people, she went forth to meet the King with the words 'And if I perish, I perish'!

This is a time of unparalleled harvest for the Kingdom of God. We are living in the computer age and an instant society. There is no more time to be passive and indifferent anymore. We need to move. But we cannot allow the excitement of the harvest and the wonder of the modern age to cloud our senses and move us too quickly until we have waited upon God for wisdom and direction.

Miriam (Ex 1:8-2:10; 15:20-21; Num 12:1-16; 20:21)

Hiltrud Mitze, in her thumbnail sketch of this young girl,

points out that Miriam's people were slaves in Egypt, cheap labourers and second class citizens. The climate of Egypt was hot and dusty, Miriam probably had to do a lot of work in their simple home - helping in cooking, carrying water, doing the laundry on the banks of the Nile, looking after her baby brother Moses when mother too had to go to work. Was Miriam despairing or giving up? This sort of background was certainly not very favourable for the personality development of a young girl. In most people, it would probably produce shyness, fear, insecurity, an inferiority complex, feelings of depression, resentment and rebellion. Not so with Miriam. Prompted by her love and discretion, she had the joy of seeing her own mother nurturing Moses - to be the man of God he became later.

Is there a parallel in the situation of many women in India today? The economic situation of the country, no jobs, low wages, lack of education and the comparison with all the material blessings of the West. The feeling 'I am only a girl', many children in one family and lots of hard work. What about us? Are we alert to things that happen around us? Do we have real love and compassion for our family and the people we live with? Can we forget ourselves and the fear of other people, even those superior to us, because we love Jesus Christ?

But not everything in Miriam's life was positive. In fact she and her brother Aaron rebelled against the spiritual authority of Moses. The root of the problem was jealousy. What a curse this is! It destroys you and hinders God's work. They wanted more power for themselves. God had to discipline them in a severe way. She was struck with leprosy. She received healing and cleansing only after she repented and Moses interceded. This shows how seriously God deals with sin of any kind. Maybe we are jealous or grumbling deep inside. Perhaps we are disobedient refusing to take a step forward in an area that the Lord has shown to us many times? Miriam's life talks about the Lord who is holy and at the same time full of grace and compassion. He who was able to use Miriam in His perfect plan for His people, can He not do the same with us?

The Value of the home and family

"But you will receive power when the Holy Spirit comes on you; and you will be my witnesses in Jerusalem, and in all Judea and Samaria, and to the ends of the earth." (Acts 1:8) It is like tossing a pebble into the lake, isn't it? We throw ourselves into being light bearers where we are and the waves we make reach far. The woman begins with her family and others close to her.

Household Salvation

Is it well with your husband, your child and different members of your family? If not, there is wonderful encouragement in the scriptures to believe that if we are faithful, God will somehow, somewhere, someday, bring them into His glorious blessing of salvation and the family circle in heaven will be unbroken. Pray for them. Pray for them without ceasing. Be an example before them of the love of Christ. Serve them and care for them. The devil loves to break up homes, but our God delights in blessing and building up families.

Do not misunderstand me. I *do* mean that each member of the family must individually repent of his/her sin and exercise faith in the atoning death of Christ the only Saviour; but if we will do our part and exercise faith for their salvation, the Lord will work upon them. If we continue to believe, eventually He will bring them into the Kingdom. What glorious possibilities there are in believing prayer! What examples from Scriptures of Noah, Hannah and Joshua, the Philippian jailer, Cornelius and their households.

Open Home

One can think of innumerable instances where women who have just come to know the Lord have led whole families to the Lord. Further, by keeping an open home, we can share our faith to all who come there. Large numbers of prayer groups are run by women in Madras. It is heard that housewives in the localities come and large numbers of them are converted. The broken and helpless too can be taken into the love and care of our home and find healing for their bodies and peace through Jesus Christ.

Witnessing in Society

Evangelism

Women in India have been described as 'the custodians of their faith'. They are the 'perpetuators of religion, culture and purity of race'. It is said that Hinduism in India stands firm on the strength of its women.

It is true we hear of the low place given to women and of the way they are treated. But this should not lead us to conclude that they have no significant role to play. They usually get their wishes carried out through the men. They are basically manipulators and not front line activists. 'Wife burning' should not lead us to think of only a cruel husband but the cruel domination of a manipulating mother-in-law is also a factor that must be taken into account.

In her paper *Expand Your Witnessing Horizons*, Lydia Sunderaraj of IMA states: "Statistics hold that 49% of Indians are female. Of the 51% of males, about one third are boys below the age of twelve. Therefore, to evangelise this 65% of Indians who live mostly in traditional societies, women are the only effective witnesses. In places like Aligarh we have found by experience that women evangelists are the only possible channel to reach the Muslim Mohallas, where no man is permitted to do evangelism. Women also have far greater communication access than men to children. Men tend to share their knowledge with the seeker whereas women share their feelings. Her child compassion can win many a seeker. Dr Nambudinipud states that 'the philosophic Hindu can stand unassailed by all our strategies of evangelism but the Hindu succumbs, defenceless in the face of divine love shown by a Christian witness.'"

Caught in the web of prostitution, unfortunate ones very soon become easy victims of a whole lot of pests starting from the landlady down to the money lenders and policemen. Physically they are dumped into such deplorable decrepit old buildings which could give way at any moment. Morally they have lost everything - even their own self respect.

As ambassadors of Christ, it is our duty therefore to take the gospel to this, so far untouched group. O that the Spirit of God will help us here to lift up our eyes to 'look at the fields! They are ripe for harvest.' (John 4:35). Jesus reminds us that the field is the world (Matt 13:38). And what do we see? How do we respond?

In India who can reach the vast multitudes of Hindu and Muslim women? Who can reach the countless women in the bondage of fear, shame and suffering? Only the Christian woman!

We live in a fragmented society. Governments fall. Families divide. Individuals are living in the fear and bondage of sin and evil. It is only the women who is becoming whole who has Good News to share with her world.

Prayer

"The greatest part of the missionary enterprise is prayer", said Dr McQuilkin. As I heard him speak earnestly and movingly on the importance of prayer, I noted with interest that of his six illustrations of prayer warriors who interceded for missions and missionaries, five of them were women! He underlined the power the women have released and are releasing from God through prayer. For prayer indeed 'moves the hand that moves the world', breaking through barriers, reconciling hardened sinners to a merciful God.

In D L Moody's time, one elderly invalid prayed and revival broke out with much power in her village and all around. Women can 'adopt' missionaries and advance the cause of missions through fervent and unceasing prayer.

The challenge of Susannah Wesley, the wonderful mother of John and Charles Wesley, is fresh before me. She was a mother of 17 children. You can well imagine the load of work she had! Yet she spent one hour each day praying for her 17 children. To her, each child was a mission field! And what strong men and women drew out of that home to the honour and glory of God and the blessing of countless men and women down the centuries.

No matter how busy we may be, we must find time to pray. Women can always make time for whatever they really want to do. 'Could you not keep watch for one hour' (Mark 14:37) comes the voice of Jesus to you and me today - that hour that can change the world for Him.

The missionary wife

Joyce Bowyers, in her article *The Role of Married Women Missionaries*, points out that the "wives of missionaries need to be encouraged strongly to develop their abilities as they often see themselves primarily as supporters and nurturers. Their role goes through drastic changes in focus as children are born, grow up, go to boarding school and eventually leave the family! The role of the married woman missionary has usually been a derived role in that it was largely defined by her husband's assignment."

Within this framework, several role patterns or 'wife styles', have emerged with many combinations and variations:

1. home maker
2. background supporter
3. teamworker
4. parallel worker

The key issue in this categorisation is not what the wife does but how she sees herself and how she is seen by her husband. It is not concerns about role recognition but more immediate and pressing problems that demand the missionary wife's attention; coping with primitive living conditions, adapting to a different culture, child rearing, etc. These issues are often ignored because they are less obvious and relate to underlying assumptions and tensions. However, failure to recognise them and deal with them often leads to low self-image and long term low grade depression which in turn contributes to health problems, marital and family stress, and tragic misuse and waste of precious human resources. The role of a missionary wife therefore needs frequent re-evaluation, re-definition and reconstruction that they can be better used.

Can we do it?

Having said all this, you may agree with me regarding the harnessing of women's potential for God's mission but you question - 'how'? As a leader, how did Hudson Taylor do it? As a pastor, how did Yonggi Cho do it? As women, how did Florence Nightingale and Amy Carmichael and Pandita Ramabhai do it?

I praise God for several leaders in Operation Mobilisation who carry deep concern for women, to see them emerge from their cocoons and develop fully and beautifully for His glory. I know pastors who also motivate the women in their churches for more active ministry. I know husbands who have been willing to stay at home and look after the children, to enable their wives to speak at a women's meeting or attend a Bible study or prayer meeting. One husband said, "I've told me wife I'll even shine her shoes if she'll go out and do something - but she will not." Another leader said, "I'm always in the limelight and I do not want my wife to be my shadow. I encourage her to develop her own gifts and ministry." At a recent women's conference I rejoiced to hear women testify they wouldn't have come if their husbands had not 'pushed' them to come! Praise the Lord for them.

My plea to pastors and Christian leaders is to consider more seriously the teaching and training of women in their congregations or care. It will be rewarding to see churches come alive. My earnest plea to husbands, for whom 'the tea tastes sweeter from my wife's hand' and who would want her in the home always to attend to her duties - to release her for Christ's sake, to learn the Word, have fellowship and develop a ministry. Don't misunderstand me. I do believe a wife's priority is her home and family. Her ministry outside is only glorifying to God when done in submission to her husband. I know far too many women who long to learn and be involved, but their husbands do not allow them.

My final plea is to you, my sisters, to 'arise and shine'. We can get blessed in a meeting. But if we do not learn something of daily discipline, we will never amount to anything for Jesus. Discipline means doing what you know you should do rather than what you feel like doing. C S Lewis, in his *Screwtape Letters* says, "We have a tendency to think and not to act. The more we feel without acting, the less we will ever be able to act, and in the long run the less we'll be able to feel."

Be available to the Lord for whatever way He pleases to use you. "For the greatest ability in God's eyes is availability", says Martha Hoke. Often I used to talk to the Lord about how I wasn't trained or adequate, brilliant or fluent. The Lord reminded me of 2 Cor 4:7 "But we have this treasure in jars of clay to show that this all-surpassing power is from God and not from us." If God wanted a beautiful, glamorous salt shaker, He would have made me differently. He wanted an earthen vessel - a plain, available container so that the attention would go to the contents, not to the container. Are you available just as you are?

Perhaps you too feel ill-equipped, unqualified! Jesus will take you and make you far more than you ever dreamed of being or doing. "I can do everything" (even witness) "through him who gives me strength." (Phil 4:13) So everywhere we go we must talk about Christ to all who will listen. Begin in your home. Talk to the servant who works for you, the milkman, newspaper man, people who come to your door. Then go out into your neighbourhood and and community telling them what Christ has done for each of them.

Jabez called on the God of Israel saying, "Oh, that you would bless me and enlarge my territory! Let your hand be with me, and keep me from harm so that I will be free from pain.". And God granted him that which he requested. (1 Chron 4:10)

If the Lord is in it, there will be painful but exciting growth and He will stretch us as He enlarges our 'coast'. He will also do the extraordinary as we allow Him to lead us one step at a time. . . knowing that He goes before.

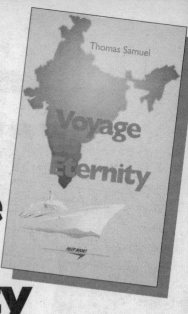

Voyage
to
Eternity

Thomas Samuel

Our life on this planet is but for a brief period. Whether rich or poor, educated or illiterate, known or unknown, we are on a journey which began on the day we were born. Like the three friends who met on a voyage, the big question is, `Do you know which way you are going'. You and I are created for eternity, but the choice we make now will determine our destiny. This book deals with life's searching questions in a most simple way. Find the answers for yourself.

Over 100,000 copies have been sold and distributed in Hindi alone and this book has also been published in three other languages, Kannada, Tamil and Malayalam.

Price £1.00 Paperback 80pp

ISBN 1 85859 007 8

PILOT BOOKS

13 Warner Road   Bromley   BR1 3RR   UK

JOHN BUNYAN'S
THE PILGRIM'S PROGRESS
IN MODERN ENGLISH

ADAPTED BY DICK WORTH

Originally written in 1678, Pilgrim's Progress is one of the greatest "classics" ever written.

Millions of copies in hundreds of editions have been printed in the last 300 years.

This latest edition in modern English makes this timeless classic suitable for all family members from grandparents down to young children.

Price £1.00 Paperback 144pp

ISBN 1 85859 003 5

PILOT BOOKS

13 Warner Road   Bromley   BR1 3RR   UK

SONG OF THE LORD CHRIST

BY DHANJIBHAI FAKIRBHAI

Following the tradition of the Hindu devotional guide, Professor Dhanjibhai Fakirbhai brings us this beautiful song of the Lord Christ.

Fifteen "Yogas" and eight discourses, all very short, easy to read and meditate on, make this an ideal book for those who want to increase their knowledge of the Divine.

Price £1.00 Paperback 128pp

ISBN 1 85859 006 X

PILOT BOOKS

13 Warner Road   Bromley   BR1 3RR   UK